This is
Practical Weather Forecasting

This is
Practical
Weather
Forecasting

Dieter Karnetzki

Adlard Coles Nautical
London

Reprinted 1994 by Adlard Coles Nautical
an imprint of A & C Black (Publishers) Ltd
35 Bedford Row, London WC1R 4JH

© United Nautical Publishers SA,
Basel Switzerland 1990

First edition published by Nautical Books 1990
Reprinted by Adlard Coles Nautical 1994

ISBN 0-7136-5701-4

Printed and bound in Italy

Translated from the German edition by Robin
Inches, MITI

Reproduction of the tables and maps on pages 9,
121, 122, 123, 124, 129, 131, 132, 133, 135, 136,
137, 138, 139, 140, 141, 142, 143, 161, 162, 163,
164, 184 by kind permission of the German
Hydrographic Institute

Drawings:
Dieter Karnetzki/Ekkehard Schonart

Photographs:
Heinrich Diessen (1), Siegfried Gliewe (1),
Dieter Karnetzki (47), Ostermayer (1), Kurt
Schubert (2), *Yacht* (6), *Yacht* – Archiv/Franz
Huber (1), *Yacht* – Archiv/L, M. Ritzi (2).

Contents

Preface

Wind and weather have always had a decisive influence on seafaring and the ever-increasing introduction of technology has not changed that in any way. On the contrary, better boats and more comprehensive equipment make it possible to undertake more and more distant cruises, which means longer periods at sea and more exposure to the vagaries of the weather. Cruises to foreign waters and strange countries bring language problems, forcing the yachtsman to take a greater interest in the subject of the weather.

Recreational navigation has indeed got easier and safer; only one thing hasn't changed: no-one can relieve the skipper of his responsibility for craft and crew. Prudence demands a solid basic knowledge of meteorology, not only for planning cruises but also for carrying them out safely. Many sailors and power-boaters have contributed to this book, by bringing me their problems and experiences. On the whole you won't find too much theory here – and I hope you won't miss it. In the creation of this book the slogan has been 'From practical experience – for practical use', and at sea the first thing you want to know is when the wind is going to shift and how strongly it is going to blow, rather than what principles of physics it obeys.

So it would give me great pleasure if this book were to become part of every on-board library, to provide on-the-spot practical assistance. I shall continue to be grateful for suggestions and reported experiences, for I believe that only if there is an ongoing dialogue, based on a common interest in recreational seafaring, between author and reader, can a book hope to be of assistance to a large number of people.

Dieter Karnetzki

Practical meteorology for our sailing waters

Weather and wind

'. . . and now, the general situation at 1900:

Low 998, Iceland, swinging eastwards, deepening. High 1028 west of Biscay, stationary, strengthening. Ridge 1015 northern Germany, swinging south somewhat, weakening. Extensive low 983 east of Lofoten, stationary, little change. Secondary depression eastern Baltic . . . Peripheral low 1010, southern Sweden, deepening . . .'

That's what comes out of the loudspeaker when the shipping forecast is transmitted. A mass of information is presented in the shortest of time – and in a language which first has to be explained to the non-meteorologist.

What really is concealed behind all those meteorological concepts with which we have to work? In a short survey, I want briefly to define and explain the necessary technical terms, and what actually constitutes weather.

Weather is the sum total of the meteorological elements effective in one place at a given time. It is a momentary event generated by individual elements such as atmospheric pressure, temperature, wind, cloud, precipitation etc. The expression 'rainy autumn weather' which can often be heard is thus not correct. Expressions such as showery weather, rainy weather or cold-front weather are less incorrect since they approximate more closely to the definition. To be absolutely correct it should be: it is raining, the air temperature is $+15°C$, visibility about 4 km, atmospheric pressure . . . etc. That would state the weather corresponding to the definition. Well, we don't necessarily want to be quite as strict (and dull) as that – but I want to explain how these notions are really defined, because only then can you use them properly.

Atmospheric condition is the *overall* character of a weather sequence. This notion is thus no longer tied to a fixed location, and it also embodies a time-span that is indirectly indicated by adjectives and adverbs. For example: autumnal atmospheric conditions; sea-influenced atmospheric conditions; persistent, cool, summer atmospheric conditions.

Climate is the *average* condition of the atmosphere over a region, considered over a long period of time, with all average and extreme components of weather as well as atmospheric conditions. Climate also includes a consideration of geographical latitude, height above sea level, distance from sea or ocean, and local peculiarities. Clearly a spot on the slope of a mountain on the side facing the prevailing wind will have a totally different climate from one similarly located but on the side shielded from the wind.

A brief explanation of the most important concepts of weather reports

The low or **depression**. A low is a region with atmospheric pressure lower than that of its surroundings. In learned circles a low is also called a 'cyclone', not to be confused with the Indian Ocean tropical revolving storms. Imagine the earth's atmosphere as a shell with dips inwards and bulges outwards. A low is like a valley in this air shell. The shell's outer surface is here *lower relative to the earth's* than elsewhere.

Depending on their size and level of weather activity, we differentiate between special forms of lows:

The trough A horizontal extension away from the centre of the low. The bad-weather zone extends in a teardrop shape from the low's core. Troughs are dangerous because they shift rapidly, give scarcely any warning and regularly bring heavy weather.

The secondary depression
This is a miniature trough. Weather activity is lower than with a full-size trough. Secondary depressions are narrow bands of bad weather running out from the core. Mostly they are weather fronts.

The peripheral low
Found on the boundary between a high and a low. It is a small low which can also be called a *wave* or *wave disturbance*.

The col
A col links two separate lows. It is also a zone of lower atmospheric pressure, but there is a limit to how bad the weather gets. Consider it as a narrow connecting-valley linking two extensive valleys (lows).

The high
A region with a higher atmospheric pressure than that of its surroundings. The correct designation is *anticyclone*. Using the picture of the air shell with dips and bulges, a region with high atmospheric pressure constitutes a bulge. The shell's outer surface is here *higher*.

The ridge
A horizontal bulge from the centre of the high that brings weather similar to that in the high. Also called a *wedge*.

The high-pressure bridge
A link between two highs. Weather phenomena are as in the high, but less pronounced.

This sample of a weather map contains all the important terms found in weather reports.

Blue = cold front

Purple = occlusion

Red = warm front

Hatched = trough

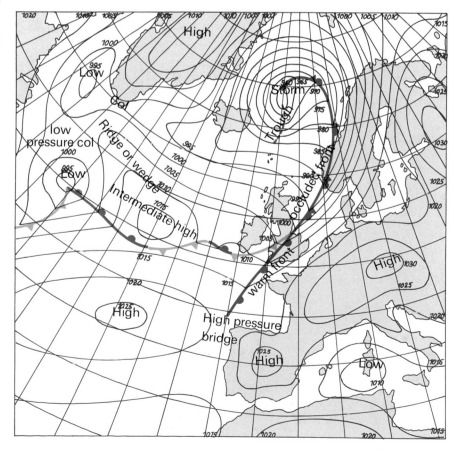

The intermediate high
These arise at the back of pronounced lows. The good weather they bring is only short-term since they nestle between two successive lows.

The fronts
Zones of bad weather connecting with low-pressure regions (see secondary depressions).
Cold fronts bring colder air with good visibility and showers from burgeoning cloud.
Warm fronts bring warmer air with poor visibility and rain from continuous cloud-cover.
Occlusions are regions where warm and cold fronts mingle and accordingly bring variable weather activity.

Circumnavigators don't care for this region at all, naming it the Doldrums, since there is either scarcely any wind and even that often changes direction. Sails can only utilise horizontal wind; air blowing upwards is useless for the propulsion of a yacht.

What happens to the air that has risen from the Equator?
If it could rise interminably we soon wouldn't have any water left on earth, and it would get colder every day because moisture and warmth would be transported into space. Fortunately the air shell has a blocking layer, at the Equator at a height of about 15 to 20 km. This blocking layer acts like a ceiling and

all upward movement stops: only sideways movement can continue, i.e. northwards or southwards to higher latitudes.

Since substantially the same processes occur in both hemispheres, we shall speak in terms of the familiar northern hemisphere. The risen air mass from the equatorial zone, the Doldrums, is transported polewards at high altitude. This brings it into cooler climatic zones on the way north, and it also cools down, becomes denser and sinks again slowly. This sinking takes place on an enormous scale, so that there is a belt of sinking air right around the earth. We call it the **subtropical high-pressure belt**. So in contrast to the Equatorial zone, where the air

The circulation of the earth's atmosphere

Behind the world-wide weather scenario there lies concealed a complex circulation of the air shell. It takes the form of several partial circulations. The evaporation and heating effect particularly strong near the Equator creates a global low-pressure belt right around the earth. In this zone the air rises to great heights because it is strongly heated by solar radiation and it also entrains a great deal of evaporated water.

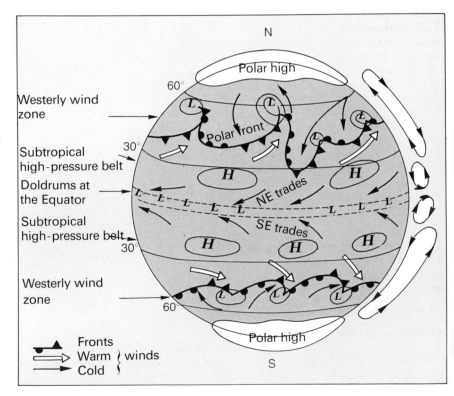

The circulation of the atmosphere

rises, we have here in the subtropics a zone of descending air.

For sailors this is of course again a zone with little wind, since no sail can convert wind blowing downwards. Already in our ancestors' time these maritime regions with calm for much of the time were christened the Horse Latitudes; some ships had to wait for wind here for such a long time that they consumed all their stores, and in the end had to resort to killing and eating the horses on board.

The air which has descended in the region of the subtropical high-pressure belt naturally has to go somewhere, and forms part of the **trade wind** circulation.

From the zone of the subtropical high which extends roughly from 20° to 40° N, the air flows back to the Equator in a layer close to the earth's surface, thus completing that circulation. This air current, which can be relied on pretty well, has been appreciated for centuries by sailors as it enabled them to cross oceans without difficulty.

Now let us make a mental leap to the North Pole, from which we want to complete the picture of the atmospheric circulation. In the polar region we find a zone of sluggish cold air, extending rather like a cap over the high latitudes. Naturally the atmospheric pressure here is higher than in other latitudes, since the air is extremely cold and thus dense. Meteorologists talk of the **Polar high**, or also of the **Arctic high-pressure region**. This extends roughly from the Pole down to 60° N.

There are thus two mechanisms that can generate a high:

The dynamic high arises from downward-flowing air, with the amount sinking from a great height always somewhat greater than what can flow away at ground level, raising the ground-level atmospheric pressure. When a dynamic high ceases to receive reinforcement from

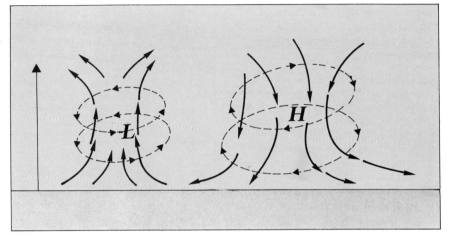

upper altitudes, it breaks down and the pressure drops.

The cold high arises from cooling (and shrinkage) of the air. For example: the Siberian anticyclone in winter. 'Thermal high' is another name for it.

You can apply the same argument to depressions:

The dynamic low is generated by upwards-flowing air, with flow away at the top always somewhat greater than re-supply from the bottom, so that the ground pressure drops.

The heat low arises from strong heating of the air layer next to the ground. The heated air expands and rises. For example: the Spanish heat-depression in summer.

Now you will ask, what exactly happens in the zone between 40° and 60° N? Intentionally, I have left consideration of this interesting zone to the end. This intermediate-latitude zone is also called the **westerlies zone** or the **westerlies belt**. European and North American weather with its unsettled character is characteristic

The circulation of the air as seen from the side. Air flows into the low, from the bottom and out again at the top. Into the high, it flows from the top, then downwards to flow out again near the ground.

Troughs and ridges

Although the boundary between cold polar air and warm tropical air is quite distinct, it is moving all the time. Warm air pushes up into the polar region, cold air into the tropics.
Below: how the interplay of polar and tropical air looks on a high-altitude weather map as produced by computer.

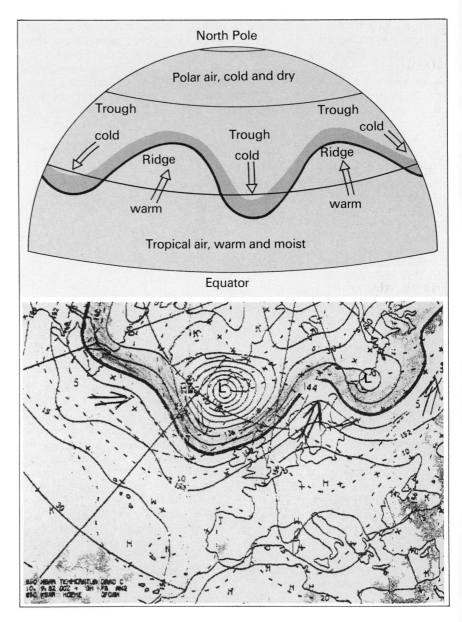

of this climatic zone. Here there is an encounter between air masses from greatly differing climatic zones. From the north, the polar cold air extends southwards, the movement reinforced by the centrifugal effect of the earth's rotation. Ranged against this is the air mass of the subtropical high-pressure belt, resisting the spread of polar air stably and immovably. Occasionally it even breaks out northwards and displaces the cold air resident there.

The intermediate latitudes are the only ones with predominantly unsettled weather, caused by those two antagonistic air masses pushing forward alternately from north and south, as they joust for supremacy over the zone.

When cold air advances south, we call that area a **trough**. When warm air advances north, it is called a **ridge** or **wedge** and is always a high-pressure area. (They extend from the subtropical high towards the Pole, i.e. from a warm region into a cooler: this reinforces the high pressure, for the subtropical warm air gets heavier as it cools.) As a general rule, high pressure wedges and ridges are fair weather regions.

Analogously, the low-pressure trough is a bad-weather zone, for air moving towards the Equator from

the Polar high is warmed, becomes lighter and thus exerts less pressure at ground level. A cold high thus turns into a warm low.

In the westerlies zone we find troughs and ridges advancing and retreating without interruption all round the globe.

12

The air mass and its front

Essentially, an air mass is distinguished by homogeneous composition, i.e. it has the same character throughout. What this character is, is determined by the region of generation of the mass. Above a desert, only hot dry air can be generated; an air mass formed over a tropical ocean will be warm and humid. On the basis of the generation region, we can define a multitude of differing but typical air masses.

If one of these masses now starts moving – say, if a ridge extends from the Azores towards Europe – it will endeavour to retain its characteristics (in this case, warmth and humidity) for as long as possible. Air masses are conservative; they are reluctant to change. An air mass pushed far away from its origin builds up a sort of protective dike for itself. On the weather map this is marked in as a **front**.

● Fronts originate when air masses are made to move.

Since an air mass need not defend its rear, it creates the protective front only ahead of it. So the fronts on a weather map are no more than the boundary lines between two different air masses. To show at once in which direction a cold front is moving, cold air masses get an acute-angled triangle; warm ones, a semicircle.

Fronts are boundaries between different air masses, so you can imagine that the power-struggles there don't remain hidden. In fact the result is always markedly active

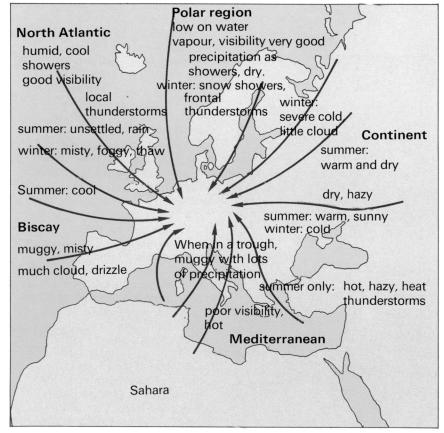

Source regions and movement of typical air masses

North Atlantic
humid, cool
showers
good visibility
local
thunderstorms
summer: unsettled, rain
winter: misty, foggy, thaw
Summer: cool

Biscay
muggy, misty
much cloud, drizzle

Polar region
low on water
vapour, visibility very good
precipitation as
showers, dry.
winter: snow showers,
frontal
thunderstorms
winter:
severe cold,
little cloud
Continent
summer:
warm and dry
dry, hazy
summer: warm, sunny
winter: cold

When in a trough,
muggy with lots
of precipitation
summer only: hot, hazy, heat
thunderstorms
poor visibility,
hot
Mediterranean
Sahara

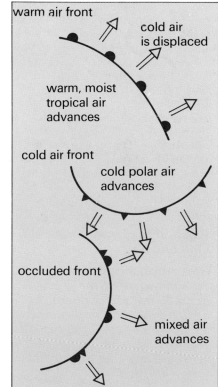

The front-linked symbols

The air mass character symbol also indicates direction of movement.

warm air front
cold air
is displaced
warm, moist
tropical air
advances
cold air front
cold polar air
advances
occluded front
mixed air
advances

13

weather. In the boundary between different air masses there is cloud, precipitation, fog, thunderstorms – in short:

● Fronts are regions of bad weather.

For the generation and activity of highs and lows with their manifold weather phenomena, forces are required. If in our daily lives we give little thought to these forces, one of the reasons is that air appears to us to be a non-entity. That this thin gas also has weight we scarcely notice, since we breathe it in and out, walk through it effortlessly and are barely conscious of it. The total weight of the air around the earth is enormous and beyond our conception. The air in the earth's shell weight 6×10^{24} kg (a 6 with 24 noughts after it) so you can imagine the sort of forces nature has to raise to move it about. In principle, air behaves rather like water. Children playing in puddles like to build connecting channels to allow the water to flow around: it will carry on flowing until the water level in all the linked puddles is the same. The reason for this levelling

Balance of pressure between high and low

High atmospheric pressure means too much air at one place in the atmosphere. As with an overflowing vessel, the air flows out towards the sides. The low lacks air compared with the high, so the air flows into it to fill it up.

If you look at this whole process from the side, the balancing happens in the same way as if water were flowing.

flow is gravity, which is permanent and tries to make all levels the same. The atmosphere is also subject to gravity, and as soon as some inequality in the shell levels arises (differing atmospheric pressures), gravity moves it towards uniformity. Only we have never had that uniform atmospheric pressure over all the earth and never will. Other forces, in conflict with gravity, prevent attainment of the stable state. Since the earth is rotating at phenomenal speed about its own axis, centrifugal forces develop which endeavour to fling everything into outer space in opposition to gravity.

Another force familiar to us from everyday life is the pressure-

High and low seen from above

Section through the air shell

earth's surface

balancing (pressure-gradient) force. The greater the level difference, the more violent the balancing process. The larger the pressure differences in the earth's air shell, the larger the force trying to balance the pressures.

There is one thing all the forces in our air shell have in common: what they cause is always movement or what we call wind. *Wind is the product of forces in the atmosphere.*

● Wind is air in motion.
Gravity causes downward wind and is thus significantly involved in the generation of high-pressure regions. **Centrifugal force** tends to transport air masses from the polar regions towards the equator, and is thus involved in extensive circulation belts (see trade winds). **Pressure-balancing** or pressure-gradient force is permanent and everywhere, and acts to establish a uniform atmospheric pressure over the whole of the globe. **Frictional force** is a component endeavouring to suppress all kinds of movement. **Inertia**, on the contrary, is a component which opposes all change. Stationary air tries to keep stationary, but by the same token air that is on the move aims to keep moving at the same speed.

The full scenario of atmospheric forces is a complex one, and as a meteorologist one has in each particular case to evaluate the individual effects of the forces involved. Some co-operate and reinforce one another, others cancel each other entirely or partially. The observer, who only sees the air in motion as the product of the multiple forces, cannot say how this motion has arisen without calculating each individual component precisely.

That has given you a brief introduction to the forces in the earth's

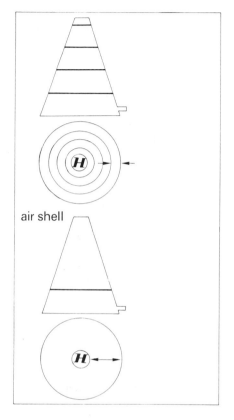

Steep gradient = isobars close together: result fast flow

air shell

Gentle gradient = isobars far apart: result slower flow

atmosphere involved in air transportation (wind) on a major scale. Before we turn to the forces which act on a minor scale – thereby causing local peculiarities – let us look at another very important force. This is the **Coriolis effect**, named after its discoverer, a French physicist. It arises from the earth's rotation and cannot itself set anything in motion, but merely deflects particles from their direction of motion as soon as they start moving.

In the normal way the air surplus to a high should flow by the shortest route into the low: that is what the forces involved are tending to achieve. If the earth did not rotate, highs and lows would indeed equalize by such a direct route. However, it is very clear from satellite photos that the Coriolis effect on the earth's atmosphere causes the air to rotate in spiral patterns.

In the northern hemisphere the air rotates spirally anticlockwise about a low, spirally clockwise about a high. In the southern hemisphere it does the opposite.

The pressure-balancing force

Imagine a conical water-container which at 5 cm intervals has rings around the outside. If this cone is filled to the top, in this example 4 rings are passed; the number of rings is a measure of the degree of filling. From a hole at the bottom, water shoots out, with a velocity proportional to the degree of filling. If in a second experiment we pour in only a little water, so that say only one ring is passed, the water will flow out at a more leisurely rate. Looking at the water cones from above you get precisely the picture shown on a weather map (here, a high). The closer together the rings (isobars) are, the more air there is pressing from above, and the more strongly the wind blows. With a low, the situation is analogous but the direction is reversed.

Europe and the Atlantic seen from the satellite

An extensive aged low is centred over the western part of the Bay of Biscay. The cloud belt of the occlusion extends from northern Spain via Ireland, France and the Gulf of Lions across to North Africa. Over the Atlantic, you can recognise the wave-form cloud cover typical of cold air.

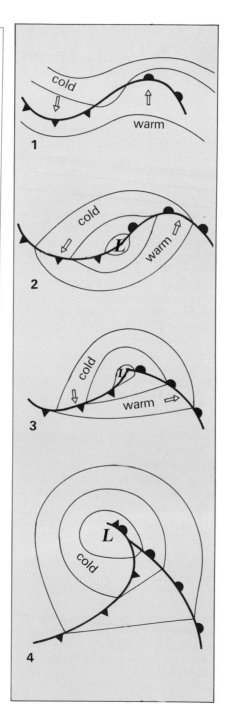

How a depression forms

**1. In the process of warm and
cold air advancing against each
other, a distinct wave has
formed in the front line.
2. This wavy front starts to
form a depression where the
cold front changes into a warm
one.
3. The low begins to swirl. The
cold front moves faster than
the warm, so the swirl
becomes self-supporting.
4. The cold front has caught up
with the warm air and an
occlusion begins to form.**

The Coriolis force is precisely nil at
the Equator and has its highest value
at the Pole. Now what is the effect of
this on the air currents in our atmosphere? Since the force does not apply
at the Equator, air movements there
are much simpler: the strength of the
wind depends only on the difference
in atmospheric pressure between high
and low. Air flow thus follows the
pattern usual for connected water
systems: it flows directly from high to
low. The direct and thus rapid
balancing of pressure differences also
prevents the generation of proper
highs and lows at the Equator.

In the polar regions the Coriolis
force attains its highest value and
thus deflects the air, which wants to
obey the pressure-balancing force,
most strongly – and so prevents the

balancing of highs and lows. In other
words:

● The closer a low or a high gets to
the Pole, the longer its life.

The development of a depression

A depression develops in the boundary region between two different air
masses. In the northern hemisphere
the two major air masses – polar cold
air from the Arctic cold-high and
warm tropical or subtropical air
from the subtropical high-pressure
zone (e.g. the Azores high) – meet
around 50° latitude.

Somewhere along the length of a
boundary surface between different
air masses, at some time, a wave will

17

form by chance because in nature such ruler-drawn boundaries have no existence – nor would they be stable if they had. Such a bulge in the air mass boundary can grow and become a rotating low. The causes cannot be explained here; but it happens often and we have discussed the forces involved. Calculation of when and where a depression arises is possible only with large computers. So, a wavy air mass front produces displaced cold air in one zone, and displaced warm air in the other. But where warm air has pushed into cold, there is now a lower pressure than before because the warm air is less dense. Where warm air advances, there must therefore be a drop in atmospheric pressure. On the other side of the wavy front, simultaneously the reverse is happening: heavy cold air displaces light warm air, so the atmospheric pressure here rises.

Out of a wavy front, dynamic behaviour of the previously balanced atmospheric pressure field has thus developed. Whether nature leaves it at that, or whether the wavy front develops into a depression, we cannot see from the normal ground-level weather maps. To assess these factors, meteorologists use 'high-altitude maps' quite unlike those you are familiar with: weather is not shown at all, but rather calculated physical quantities relating to the atmosphere.

But let us get back to how a depression develops. Assuming that conditions in the atmosphere are favourable to the generation of a low, our wavy front will carry on developing. The next event is the start of upward movement of the air at the pivot point of the wavy front.

I'm sure you will have noticed that in dealing with the process of wave formation there has not so far been any mention of such upward movement, which after all is a characteristic of a fully developed low. It is the theoretical calculations by the meteorologists and their computers, concerning the high-altitude layers above the wave, which indicate whether all the other conditions are favourable to the air there being lifted. As a product of the two separate components of motion – advancing air masses and lift at the centre – a joint rotary motion is now generated. While the two air masses revolve about the centre, the air is lifted, with always more carried away from the top than can flow in at the bottom. As a result, ground-level pressure drops, and the low deepens. Imagine the motive power for a depression as a sort of atmospheric vacuum cleaner at a height of 8 to 10 km and drawing the air upwards.

In the development of a low, we can consider two separate processes:
1. The movement of the air mass boundaries (fronts) which inter-swirl;
2. The behaviour of the atmospheric pressure.
● As a consequence of its deepening, the strength of the wind in the whole of the low increases, since the rate of air movement depends directly on the magnitude of the atmospheric pressure difference.

Now it is time to define a further essential concept.
● **Isobars** are lines of constant atmospheric pressure.
Exactly as you can make a circuit of a hill (or a valley), while remaining at precisely the same height, so it is with atmospheric pressure in the case of highs and lows. If you think of some pressure value outside that at the core of the depression, you can make a circuit (mentally) around this at that value. The path you follow is an isobar. That there can be only one path with that value will be obvious to you from the hill and valley analogy: even a single step upwards and you are at a greater height than before; a tiny step downwards equally results in an immediate departure from the desired value. And when you have completed a circuit at a constant level, you must be back exactly where you started from.

This allegory from land topography can be applied logically to atmospheric pressure and the isobars without any difficulty: isobars are lines forming closed loops and accurately indicate a unique value of atmospheric pressure. They link all the points where that pressure exists.
● Isobars cannot cross or intersect (for then there would be two different atmospheric pressures at one and the same point). The figures alongside the isobars on weather maps indicate the pressure value in Hectopascals (hPa) or millibars (mb).

The formation of a cold front

If cold air pushes in underneath warm, the latter must move upwards. Since the slope of the cold-air wedge is pretty steep, the upward movement of the warm air is correspondingly rapid. The result is the formation of clouds: air forced upwards cools, since the farther we go from the earth's surface the colder it gets. The typical cloud form for cold fronts is heaped Cumulus. This is an indicator of turbulent upward movement and of powerful and rapid lifting processes. Just the look of the massive cumulus clouds gives the impression of concentrated energy.

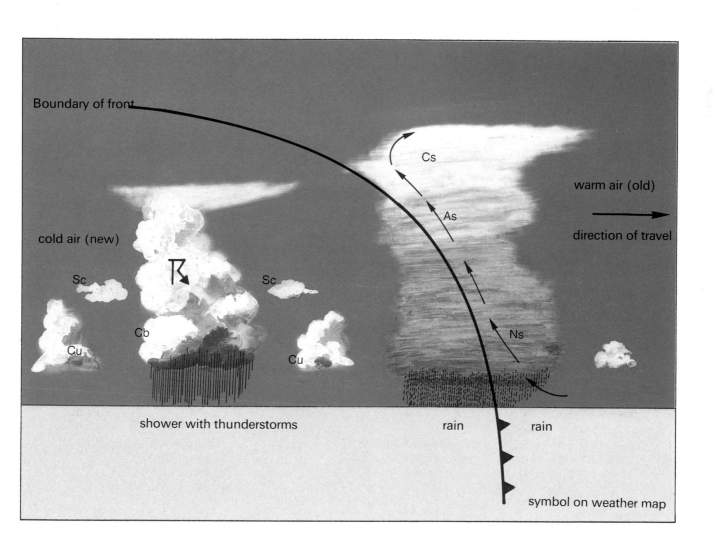

Boundary of front

cold air (new)

warm air (old)

direction of travel

Sc

Cs

As

Sc

Cb

Cu

Ns

Cu

shower with thunderstorms

rain

rain

symbol on weather map

Cross-section of a cold front

The cold front pushes forward like a roller and displaces the warmer air in front of it, lifting it powerfully in the process.
Sc = Stratocumulus
Cu = Cumulus
As = Altostratus
Cb = Cumulonimbus
Ns = Nimbostratus
Cs = Cirrostratus

Characteristic signs when a typical cold front passes

	Ahead of the front	*In the front*	*Behind the front*
Cloud	Low continuous cloud, stratus and stratocumulus	Nimbostratus, nesting cumulus, some with cumulonimbus	Cloud separating individual cu, cu-nim. with stratocumulus
Weather phenomena	Fog banks possible, starting to rain	Heavy rain, partly with thunder, later showers	Isolated showers, gusty
Wind	Direction, strength roughly constant	Vigorous increase, gusts; direction variable	Veers up to 180°, weakens temporarily; very gusty
Temperature	Constant	Dropping somewhat	Dropping a lot
Humidity	High	Dropping somewhat	Air drying quickly
Visibility	Moderate, poor in parts due to fog	Moderate, poor in showers	Improving quickly to v. good
Atmospheric pressure	First constant or falling slightly, then strong fall	Constant	Rising moderately to strongly

Characteristic signs when a typical warm front passes

	Ahead of the front	*In the front*	*Behind the front*
Cloud	Developing cirrus then altocumulus, altostratus thickening; ceiling coming down	Clouded over with nimbostratus, stratus	Clouded over, stratus or stratocumulus
Weather phenomena	Halo with thin cirrus; later coronae around moon, sun; then light rain	Precipitation strengthens, then ceases; fog/mist may follow	Fog patches, some drizzle (both only in the spring)
Wind	Increases steadily, backs somewhat	Freshens strongly, veers a bit	Strength, direction constant
Temperature	Rising	Goes on rising	Constant
Humidity	Increases noticeably	Very high	High
Visibility	Worsens steadily	Poor to fog	Moderate
Atmospheric pressure	Drops steadily	Dropping only very slightly or constant	Constant or dropping slightly

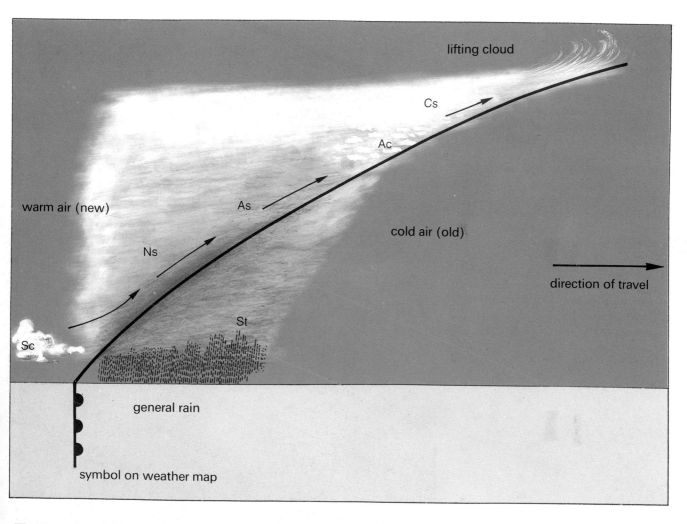

lifting cloud

Cs

Ac

warm air (new)

As

cold air (old)

Ns

direction of travel

St

Sc

general rain

symbol on weather map

The formation of a warm front

There really is no need to differentiate especially between the formation of a cold and a warm front, for where there is the one there is also the other. Whether a front has 'cold' or 'warm' characteristics depends purely on which air mass displaces the other.

When explaining the cold front, we started with the assumption that the cold air displaced the warm. But the warm tropical air can be the stronger. The initial situation is the same, but the result totally different: the less dense, warm air is incapable of pushing in underneath the cold as the less dense medium always floats on top of the other. The warm air therefore slides upwards on the cold, the latter very gradually retreating in the upper reaches. The cold air at ground level follows only much later. A well-marked warm front may have a slope up to 1000 km long; the cold

Section through a warm front

The warm air glides upwards on the cold, which deforms into a wedge shape and is pushed back slowly.

Satellite-photo of an old low

This photo was taken from an altitude of about 1500 km. The spiral structure of the depression, centred over the Arctic Ocean shows up clearly. The snow covered Norwegian coastal mountain range with its innumerable fjords is easily visible (from bottom left to right, right across the picture; Norway lies crossways). The belt of cloud running from the centre is the front cloud. Where the belt reaches Norway, it thickens: here a wave is forming from which a new low will develop. From satellite photos such important developments can be recognised as soon as they start.

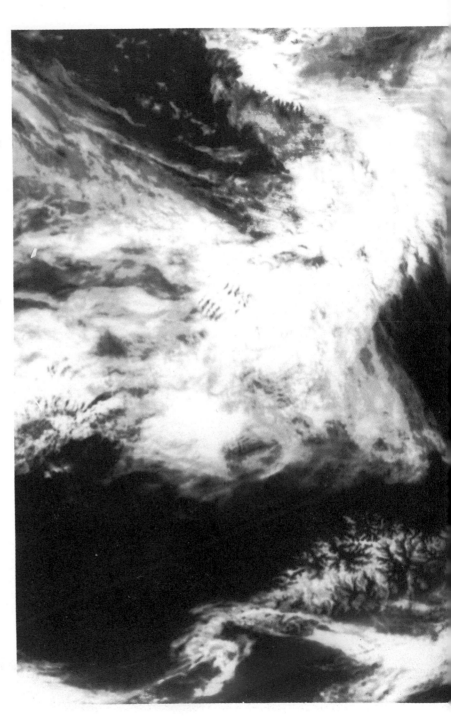

air lies underneath it like a flat wedge and retreats slowly.

Reflecting the slow and balanced movement at a warm front, the atmosphere in this region is stable. You can see this from the clouds, which almost unnoticed sit above the earth like an umbrella; they are called layer clouds (stratus). Since the warm air slides up to great heights (max. over 10 km), it gives rise to layer clouds at all three levels. The air is also cooled to such an extent that the moisture in it condenses and rain forms in the clouds, so that ahead of warm fronts there can be prolonged and evenly falling rain.

The occlusion of warm and cold fronts

The swirling interaction of fronts is due to the ground/air friction characteristics of the different air masses. Warm air moves across the earth like a doughy mass; cold air is internally very turbulent and the friction at the earth's surface is substantially lower so it advances more rapidly than the warm air – even if both are being propelled with the same amount of force.

As soon as a properly rotating low with fronts has been formed, the cold front thus starts catching up on and assimilating the warm front running ahead of it. Mixing always starts at the pivot-point, initially in the centre of the low, called the occlusion point. As the low gets older, it occludes; its fronts close up and intermingle. In the process the occlusion point first wanders away from the core, and some time later the mixed or occluded front starts winding itself at an ever increasing distance around that core, due to the centrifugal forces which continuously act on the air masses.

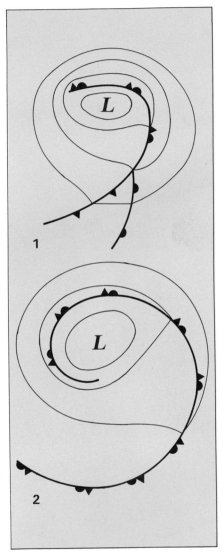

1

2

The swirling interaction of warm and cold fronts

1. The fronts are extensively occluded or mixed, starting from the centre of the low. 2. The low's swirl is fully developed. The aged front forms a wide spiral around it.

Forecasting details of the weather phenomena associated with an occlusion is far from easy. The boundary regions of the mixed air masses sometimes demonstrate more or less typical cold front characteristics, at other times behave almost like warm fronts.

Typical weather conditions in the European summer season

Even if in our latitudes (except in the Mediterranean) the weather is changing all the time, we do know of very typical weather situations which generate comparable atmospheric conditions in parts of the region. The concept of **macroweather** is at the back of this, and the term designates a type of weather where the same atmospheric conditions predominate for several days over a substantial area. These atmospheric conditions are strongly influenced by the air mass, so for our purposes we can group them into three types:

- Zonal flow type
- Meridional flow type
- Mixed flow type

Zonal flow weather

By this we mean the flow of an air mass along the same latitude, east or west from one climatic zone into another. For the North Sea and Baltic this means essentially a westerly transporting individual low-pressure regions with their weather fronts eastwards. Typical of zonal currents is the **westerly flow**. In summer Atlantic lows travel via Scotland and southern Scandinavia to Russia. The fronts are often only weak but mostly brush the North Sea and the Baltic (see map on p. 29).
Weather peculiarities
Around the coast it is unsettled and variable, mild, cool at times, rarely warm in spite of sunshine, rain and a lot of wind. On the inland lakes, winds light, but heavy precipitation with thunderstorms.

Meridional flow type

Stable high-pressure formations which bring lasting good weather are typical of meridional flows. Depending on which side of the high you are, it can be either a pure northerly or a pure southerly airstream. During the summer months only northerlies are typical; they occur most frequently in early summer. If, for instance, the Azores high transfers to the British Isles and firmly settles there, meteorologists refer to a blocking high. The enormous high-pressure region blocks the movement of the Atlantic disturbances from the west and ensure continuous good summer weather for Northern Europe.
Weather peculiarities
A lot of sunshine, little cloud. Pleasantly warm with gentle northerly winds; heat not oppressive. If a small low develops over southern Sweden, the North Sea coast and the Kattegat run the risk of strong winds, sometimes even gales – so keep an eye on what is happening in the Baltic and environs, even if that's not where you are. Good visibility with northerly winds, scarcely any fronts, precipitation rare.

Mixed flow type

This conceals weather systems which bring us older and modified air masses. Examples are northwesterly and southwesterly flows, where subtropical and maritime polar air masses mix.

The northwesterly flow is an uncomfortable type of weather for water sports, as the atmosphere pulls out all those stops that we'd rather do without in summer. Usually there is an extensive low covering Scotland, the North Sea and Scandinavia. On its western flank cold air flowing in leads to an irregular pattern of fronts building up which cause plenty of rain and wind.
Weather peculiarities
Cool verging on cold, lots of showers and gusty strong wind around the coast and in the North Sea. Signifi-

25

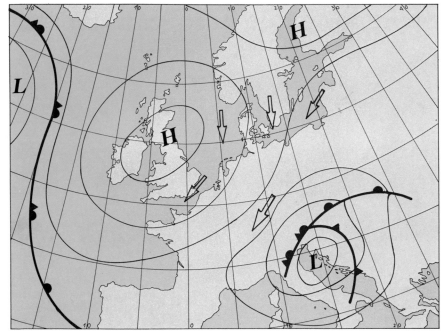

Typical summer situation, with a high over the British Isles.

cantly better weather in the Baltic, good visibility everywhere.

Southwesterly flow indeed brings warm air from the Biscay area into the English Channel and North Sea, but it stays only moderately warm because there is very little sunshine.
Weather peculiarities
Unsettled, rainy, weather; continuous high humidity. Lots of wind on the coast, frequent fog particularly in early summer.

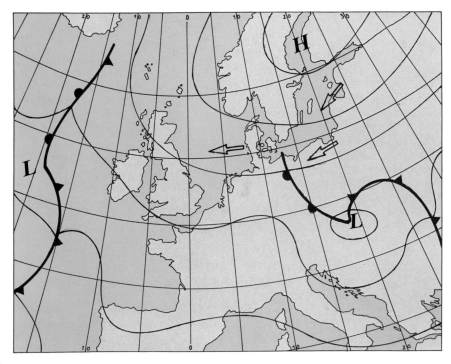

Typical stable high-pressure situation, with a high over Scandinavia.

Practical rules for weather forecasting on board

Relying entirely on official weather reports and forecasts can occasionally mean being badly left in the lurch. Increasingly, all of use are losing the skill of keeping a sharp eye on Nature and understanding her hints - of which there are plenty. Weather rules properly applied are excellent means for seeing through Nature's tricks. They don't need electricity and don't break down: you just have to keep your eyes open.

In this chapter I want to introduce a selection of weather rules, by means of examples. All have one thing in common: they are based on the laws of physics and thus can be relied on.

Wind rules

Locating the centre of a low

> *If you stand with your back to the wind, low pressure is on your left and high on the right.*

Using this rule, Buys Ballot's Law, you can judge the displacement of highs and lows, and from this possible changes in wind direction and strength.

Judging the track of a low
In the morning, stand with your back to the wind to give you a bearing for

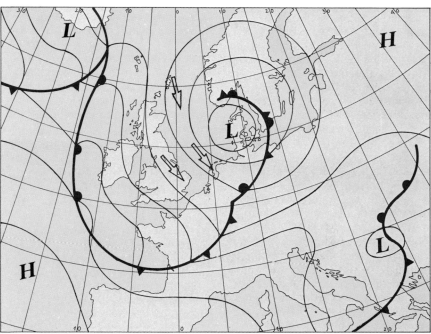

Typical NW wind situation, bringing lots of rain and strong wind.

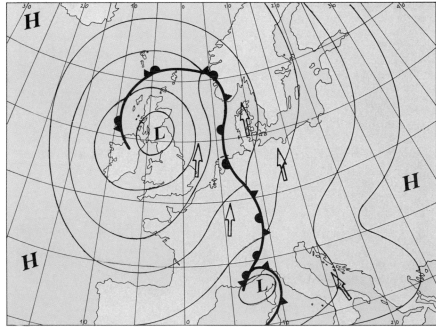

SW to S wind situation; brings cloudy, reasonably warm air.

27

the centre of the low, indicated by your extended left arm. Bearing and wind are sketched-in roughly on the chart. A few hours later, take that bearing again and get a second line for it. Now, is that second line displaced clockwise from the first, or anticlockwise?
● Clockwise rotation means that the low is going to pass with its centre to the north of you.
● Anticlockwise rotation means that the low will pass south of you.
● A steady bearing means either that the low is stationary or that its centre is heading straight for you. The barometer will tell you which, if you have been noting the trend of its readings.

Now take into account the direction of rotation of the wind around a low. A low passing to the north of you (clockwise bearing rotation) brings first southerly and then westerly winds. The further you remain from the centre region (compare on-board barometric pressure with that from the shipping report) the

weaker will be the wind and the lower the weather activity at the front.

A low passing south of you (anticlockwise bearing rotation) initially brings southerly winds, later easterly to northerly. Where the low is 'young' you may be spared weather fronts altogether since these are only to be found south of the centre; they extend north of it only when its swirl pattern is properly established.

> Note:
> *Clockwise bearing rotation = veering wind.*
> *Anticlockwise bearing rotation = backing wind.*
> *Steady bearing = strengthening wind with dropping atmospheric pressure.*

Steady winds in the North Sea and Baltic

Easterly winds indicate a stable weather situation, i.e. wind from this direction can be expected to continue for some time. At the back of this is the stable high centred over Scandinavia. If such a high is mentioned in the weather report, you can afford to plan some days ahead. Statistics indicate that the tendency for this weather to continue increases if it has already lasted some days.

Change after a period of fine weather

The changeover from a lengthy period of fine weather is almost always to a lengthy period of bad weather. The prevailing winds will then be southerly to westerly, bringing extensive precipitation.

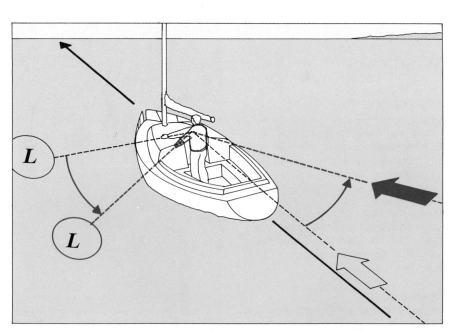

The second (red) set of arrows show that the wind has backed, shifting counterclockwise from its original direction (black). The low's centre will now pass south of the yacht.

Wind backing rapidly

This brings an equally rapid improvement in the weather, but take care: it is deceptive and short-lived. After a wet day the barometer rises steadily. There is only a mild breeze and the cloud is breaking with blue sky and lots of sun. Enjoy these hours of fine weather, but start preparing vessel and crew for bad weather now for it will be with you in about 12 hours' time. Even while the fine conditions are still with you, the barometer will start to fall again. Now watch the direction of the wind, for after a calm pause it will strengthen somewhat and back distinctly (to around south to southeast). Keep on casting an eye to the west, where a fine veil of cloud appears gradually. Like a continuous ceiling, this very high cirrus advances and means a warm front is approaching.

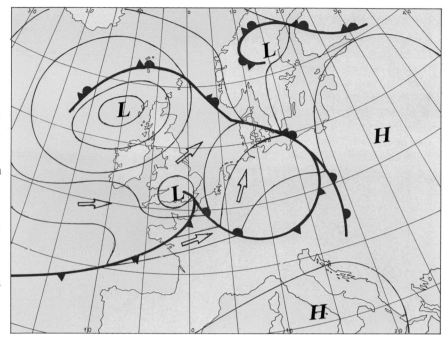

This westerly wind situation is characteristic of a frequent type of weather in the North European summer. The central low near Scotland steers minor lows past its southern flank and across northern Europe.

Visibility rules

Highs and lows transport enormous air masses worldwide, taking them to zones far from where they were generated. These air masses have certain characteristics which they surrender only hesitantly. Tropical air is warm and moist; transported to Europe it cools very gradually. This increases the relative humidity and the air becomes misty, even fog is a possibility. The high over the European continent accounts for a different situation: easterly winds bring air from the continent which is dry but heavily dust-laden. The result of several days of easterly wind is familiar: though there is no precipitation and the sun is blazing in a blue sky, visibility is poor.

Visibility improves

If, after a quiet spell of fine weather with easterly winds and the inevitable haze, visibility improves steadily, that is an infallible sign of worsening weather. What is behind this? An air-mass change is in prospect, which is gradual and therefore often overlooked. Atmospheric pressure falls slowly but steadily: a low is approaching which is bringing a general change.

Haziness increases

If during a calm spell it becomes increasingly hazy in the afternoon, thunderstorms are indicated. Over land they will develop in the late afternoon; over the sea, in the second half of the night.

Approach of a warm front

1

1. In the middle of a nice spell under the influence of an intermediate high, slowly development cirrus indicates an early deterioration of the weather.
2. In the afternoon the cloud cover slowly thickens; the cirrus comes closer, looking like a screen.

2

Stars twinkle strongly

Noticeably strong twinkling of the stars is an indication of the imminent end of a period of fine weather. Approaching cold air in the upper atmosphere produces this high-grade visibility. This air mass is exceptionally dry and clean, thence the clear stars.

Good visibility in the autumn

In the autumn just as in summer, easterly winds bring steady weather, however with very good visibility. The relatively cool continental air then warms up over the still-warm sea and the water in the air evaporates.

Poor visibility after rain

Normally visibility improves significantly after rainfall because it washes the dirt out of the air. However, if visibility remains poor after rain, there isn't going to be the usual improvement: indeed there could be worse to come. In summer you can then count on getting showers and thunderstorms.

Changes in appearance of the sun and moon

By their colourful display, the sun and moon provide a picture of the atmosphere, and they are also reliable indicators of impending changes. Apart from noting colour, watch for another optical phenomenon, the halo, usually a bad-weather

Halo and mock sun

1. Halo phenomena are always harbingers of bad weather. The coloured rings around the sun announce the approach of a rainy front.

sign. Coloured rings around the sun and the moon, extending in a wide arc across the sky, are quite frequent. Sometimes you can observe coloured or white pillars of light, and seeing two or perhaps even three suns in the sky instead of the usual one does not mean at all that you have had one too many. The optical qualities of the atmosphere permit all those curiosities to appear in our sky. There are more than a dozen halo phenomena, some of them admittedly pretty rare. Those most frequently observed are rings around

the sun and the moon, those around the sun being mostly coloured and those around the moon usually white. There can also be a smaller mock sun to the left and right. With luck, one can experience a display of the whole range of atmospheric phenomena. Opposite the sun, near the other horizon, there is an anti-sun. There may also be geometrical rings and arcs.

How do all these come about? All of them owe their genesis to the refraction and reflection of light on ice crystals in the atmosphere. High cirrus 6 to 12 km up is involved in halo generation. At those heights the temperature is $-40°-60°C$, so that the entire moisture content is ice. The cloud must be thin enough for the light to be able to penetrate it, or there would be no halo. Most often the cirrus is so thin that it isn't

2. After the halo rings around
the sun have disappeared
again, because the cloud has
thickened, you can still just see
a mock sun off to the right of
the real sun, which itself has
become diffuse. Behind it you
can already see thick cloud. The
rain will start in 6–12 hours'
time.

3. The front-associated cloud
is coming closer all the time.
Now you see a complete ceiling
of cirrus which the sun can just
about penetrate. Lower down,
altocumulus has already
pushed in, which means the
sun is going to disappear soon
and rain is not far off.

2

3

noticed, which is precisely when the finest effects appear.

Light rays can be refracted by ice crystals, as everyone knows from the glass prism. Because the crystals have a strictly geometrical shape, white light passing through them is dispersed into its spectral colours, as when water drops produce a rainbow. Each ice crystal disperses the white light on its way down to earth. Depending on whether the rays are diffracted just once or more often by the ice particles, the most varied pattern of arcs and mock suns results. Individual haloes can overlap, because the ice crystals can assume different forms: hexagonal prisms predominate, but ice discs and other forms also occur. Depending on the proportions of the different forms, the various effects appear.

● A halo in a stable high-pressure situation in summer, where the thinnest of cirrus veils forms in the sky, means: the weather situation remains unchanged.

● If after a period of fine weather cirrostratus appears – the fine grey veil in the atmosphere – and a halo forms, but after an interval disappears again, that is a sure sign of an early deterioration in the weather. The cloud thickens: the sun penetrates only diffusely, its rim no longer clearly visible. As things progress the sun disappears entirely and the cloud thickens further: there is a warm front approaching with rain not far away.

The colour of the sun

Normally the sun is red when it sets and yellow to orange in the morning. If it appears in these colours, that tells you that the atmosphere holds no threat of a weather disturbance and the weather should stay stable and fine.

> Red sun at night, sailors
>   delight;
> Red sun in the morning,
>   sailors take warning.

If the evening sun instead of being red is yellow to greyish-white, this is due to a substantial increase in the moisture in the air. Since warm air has a particularly high moisture content, we can foresee from the changed colour of the evening sun the approach of a warm front which in fact won't be with us for another whole day.

In the morning the situation is reversed: normally, because of the air's cooling down, humidity is especially high – thence the sun's yellow colour. Blood-red morning sun thus means particularly pure and unusually dry air: behind this is cold air, announcing an early deterioration of the weather.

'Red sun at night'

If the evening sun takes on a red coloration, and the whole sky even becomes luminous, that's an indication of good weather.

Red evening-sky after sunset

You can confidently reckon on good weather tomorrow.

Pale evening sun

This sunset has a yellowish-grey coloration. The build-up of cirrostratus is already clearly visible: tomorrow morning it will be raining.

1

Aureoles and rings around the moon

Sometimes on a clear night you see the moon shining progressively more diffusely and the sky around it also beginning to shine with a diffuse white light. This is called a moon aureole. Alert observers will often see coloured rings around the moon before this aureole; the two phenomena are connected and forecast a rapid worsening of the weather. The coloured rings are generated by developing cirrus (like a halo). As the cirrus cover thickens, the moon and its aureole still shine through it diffusely until it is finally totally obscured. The low-lying cloud will build up rapidly and you won't have to wait much longer for the rain.

2

Sunrise

1. If the weather is to remain settled, the sun must look yellow in the morning and turn white quickly, as soon as it has risen above the early morning mist and cloud layer.

2. This sunrise threatens early worsening of the weather, since although the sun is already quite high there is still a luminous red sky.

Yellow sun with morning dew

If the morning sun is yellowish in colour and the boat is covered in dew, you can safely assume that the day's weather will be fine. The moisture from the air which has condensed on the boat indicates that the lower atmosphere has stabilized, i.e. a high pressure system has asserted its authority. There will be little or no wind that day.

Special rules for the Mediterranean:

If an early morning look at the sky shows an unbroken ceiling of dark clouds hanging threateningly low, that is a good sign – particularly if the boat is wet with dew. These low, blackish-grey clouds, which in the North Sea and the Baltic would be cause for considerable concern, in the Med often form over the sea. The moisture in the air, condensing in cloud droplets, accumulates hundreds of metres up and forms a

Black early-morning cloud in the Mediterranean

If the early-morning sky in the Med has this sort of threatening look, don't worry – it's going to be a lovely day.

stable cloud ceiling which dissolves rapidly after sunrise. First a yellowish sun shines through; soon after, the sky is blue again, it's calm and a sunny day.

Changes in atmos-pheric pressure

A barometer is an indispensable aid for getting to grips with the weather. It is absolute nonsense for some skippers to claim that one look at the barometer is enough to 'know what's going on', even if there should be an old sea-captain somewhere who has produced good weather forecasts on that basis all his life.

The barometer shows nothing more than the *present* atmospheric pressure, and the value of that pressure has nothing to do with the present weather, let alone that to come. With low pressure at its lowest you can experience blazing sunshine, just as you can miserable rain or thunder in a powerful high. The only permissible use of atmospheric pressure for making deductions regarding weather is to provide a measure of its rate of change. The length of time a pressure change takes is decisive: the more rapid and the greater this change, the quicker and more emphatic will be that in the weather.

● Slow but continuous fall in pressure brings a change in the weather that will persist.

When a longish period of fine weather is approaching its end, this shows up on the barometer by a steady reduction of the high pressure. Then either an extensive major low is approaching from the Atlantic, bringing a period of changeable weather, or a whole family of minor lows is about to pass in quick succession over NW Europe – a typical summer weather system for the British Isles, North Sea and Baltic.

● Short-term atmospheric pressure changes bring unsettled weather.

Whether this consists of strong wind, fog, or rain, it is rare for these to persist for longer than half a day if the pressure keeps on rising and falling. Behind this is the classic westerlies sytem with lows passing in quick succession over northern and western Europe. Between the rain belts of two successive lows there is always a sunny day, courtesy of the intermediate high. So the weather sequence is: one day rain – one day sunshine – one day rain, like the barometer going continuously up and down. An impending change can be recognized by an overall tendency to rise superimposed on the continuous rise and fall of pressure. Things will soon get more settled.

● Slowly and steadily rising pressure brings a lasting improvement in the weather. This is an indication of an approaching high. The slow and continuous pressure rise shows that it must be a very large (thus stable) high, bringing a longer period of fine weather but little wind.

● Strongly rising pressure brings strong wind or a gale. Sunshine

Westerlies situation

How it looks on the barograph: atmospheric pressure is going up and down continuously; the fronts are clearly marked, cold fronts generally more clearly than warm ones.
WF = warm front,
CF = cold front

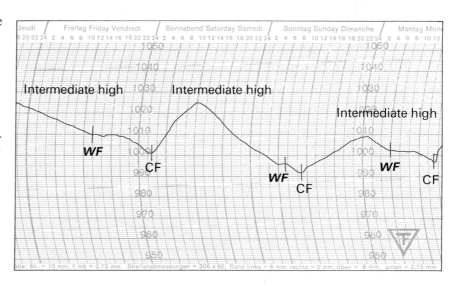

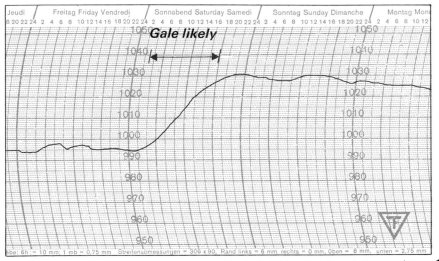

Gale likely

1050
1040
1030
1020
1010
1000
990
980
970
960
950

be: 6h := 10 mm; 1 mb = 0,75 mm   Streifenabmessungen = 306 x 90, Rand links = 6 mm. rechts = 0 mm, Oben = 8 mm, unten = 2,75 mm

Situation 1:
first rain, then wind

Ahead of the rain belt you are, in a manner of speaking, running along an isobar and so pressure remains substantially constant. The isobar spacing being constant, there won't be any change in the wind strength either. However, beyond the end of the rain belt the pressure rises rapidly if you carry on sailing across the weather map. The isobars are jammed close together and the wind is definitely stronger.

The high-pressure gale

If the atmospheric pressure starts to rise strongly, as shown here, that usually means a gale is coming. A rise-rate of more than 1 mb pr hour is a pretty sure sign.

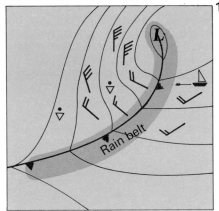

1

Rain belt

Situation 2:
first wind, then rain

If you sail across this weather map in the same way, the scenario is different. During the approach to the front the pressure will fall, since you are moving roughly at right angles to the isobars and towards the low pressure. Because of the close isobar spacing wind force will increase rapidly. Close to the front, rain will start. The strong wind stays on, but as soon as the front has passed the rain will stop suddenly, breaks appear in the cloud and the wind drops noticeably = pressure and wind then remain pretty steady. The weather then remains friendly and quiet apart from occasional showers.

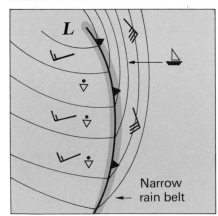

2

Narrow
rain belt

38

entices one to neglect or overlook the barometer. Even if there doesn't seem to be any change in the sky, you should turn your thoughts to strong winds if the pressure is rising strongly. Particularly in summer in the North Sea and the Baltic, these high-pressure gales, which for several days bring a lot of wind with a brilliant blue sky, occur several times.

Rules for wind and rain

Weather fronts follow differing scenarios. Sometimes it rains at first and then the wind freshens, at others it happens the other way round. Nevertheless there are some well-established rules.

> *Rain first, wind last*
> *lash up everything fast.*
> *Wind first, then rain*
> *skipper can relax again.*

Marked rainy zones are always tied to bad-weather fronts: either it rains ahead of the front or actually in the front region. The third option, that precipitation falls only behind the front, is also possible but rarer. If in your mind you travel across the two weather maps opposite, those two weather rules will be explained.

Assessing weather fronts

In the European climatic zone the bad-weather centres are the fronts, the majority extending for thousands of kilometres away from low centres. It is only rarely possible to deduce from a weather map how active an individual front is. Some rules based on experience will help.

● Slow-moving cold fronts often have a wide rain belt.

With this type of front, the rain only starts behind it. A slow boat then remains in the dirty weather longer, particularly if it's sailing in the same direction as the movement

1. First rain, then wind
The weather sequence is:

	Ahead of the front	*As it passes*	*Behind the front*
Atmospheric pressure	minimally falling or constant	rises somewhat	rises strongly
Rain/cloud	starts	stops	cloud breaks up
Wind	unchanged	veering	strengthens rapidly; strong wind or gale

2. First wind, then rain
The weather sequence is:

	Ahead of the front	*As it passes*	*Behind the front*
Atmospheric pressure	falls strongly	slowly falling or constant	little change
Rain/cloud	cloud thickens, later quickly; rain	rain stops, some showers	a few showers, cloud breaks up
Wind	increases continuously, quickly	veering squally	direction steady; dropping quickly

of the front. Thus one can easily get the impression that the weather is not changing at all. After the front has passed (recognized by the wind rotating and the barometer rising) the expected improvement doesn't happen. The typical front-following weather, which provides good sailing, holds off.

● Fast-moving cold fronts often don't have a coherent rain belt.

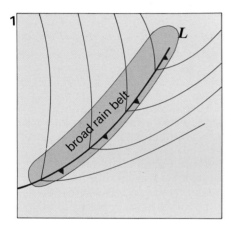

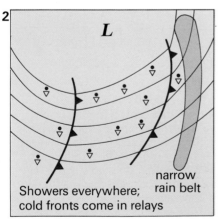

1. **Slow-moving fronts tend to have a pretty broad rain belt.**
2. **No more than a narrow rain belt, ahead of the front, is typical of fast-moving fronts.**

Cold fronts moving at more than 15 to 20 knots push well ahead of them the sort of weather which one expects to meet behind them: heavy showers with gusts. Thus one is inclined to consider the front as passing, much too soon. Take another look at the barometer: it is still falling, so the gusty front is still on the way.

The weather stays the same for quite a long time, though the front is fast-moving. Only when the pressure rise has been effective for a considerable period does the wind drop noticeably and the gusts become less fierce. If the weather forecast talks of fast-moving cold fronts, or even of cold-front sequences, you now know what this means: a lot of wind for a long time, accompanied by heavy showers and wind rising to gale or some severe gale force gusts. In this sort of weather gusts tend to be long-lasting; not infrequently a single blast can last 10 to 20 minutes and the sea will become visibly rougher.

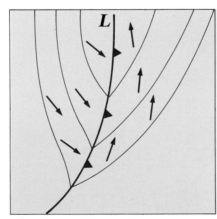

Strongly-active front

Isobars bend strongly at the front, indicating marked change of wind direction.

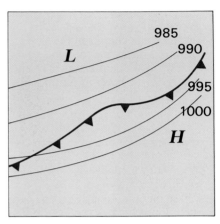

Stationary front

How the weather map looks when the front has become stationary. There are next to no bends in the isobars. Often, the front runs parallel to them.

The isobar-kink at the front

The sharper a kink there is in the isobars at a front, the more pronounced will be the front-associated weather phenomena – and the changes in the weather brought along by the front. In the case of really marked fronts, wind shift can reach 180°. If on top of that the wind is strong enough, dreadful cross-seas result.

The frontal calm

Quite often the wind in the immediate proximity of a cold front dies down noticeably and there is a tendency to disbelieve the warning in the latest shipping bulletin. The warning of strong winds seems a bit previous: something like a flat calm is spreading. Woe betide him who is deceived by this! It is true that there is a distinct spreading of the isobars in the immediate frontal region, which causes the wind to drop, but a glance at the weather map to the west shows that these same isobars later close up again surprisingly.

● Calm at a cold front most often is only the calm before the storm.

Once the front has passed, the wind veers, drops noticeably and the barometer shows the pressure rising only slightly. Don't let this weather phase mislead you; watch the pressure. Only if it keeps rising *slowly* can

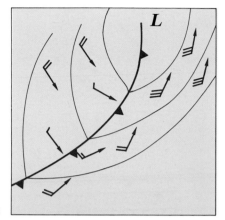

The calm front

Round the front the isobars fan out, hence the noticeable drop in wind. But keep an eye on the closing-up of the isobars further behind: there the wind will strengthen again.

Below: a typical shower cloud associated with a well developed cold front. Heavy precipitation means a drastic reduction in visibility.

you relax safely; often this quiet weather phase behind the front is only short-lived. If the pressure suddenly starts rising more steeply than before, the wind is going to strengthen *rapidly* and veer even further. Strong winds are then in the offing.

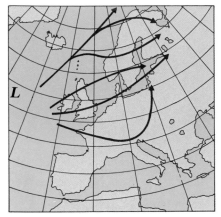

The principal lines of travel of European lows in summer.

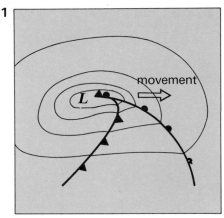

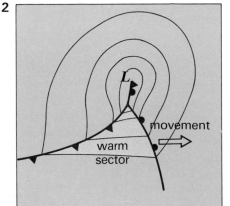

Lines of travel of lows

1. If the core of the depression has a distinctly oval shape, its direction of travel is usually along the oval's major axis.
2. 'Young' depressions often travel in the direction of the straight isobars in the warm sector between the fronts. Should the two rules be in conflict, this one wins.

Rules for the displacement of lows

Every depression has its own life cycle and moves in accordance with individual rules only rarely detectable from the weather map by non-meteorologists. The physical mechanisms vary; the trick is to discover which is dominant at the time. For classical macroweather patterns it is quite possible to indicate some principal depression tracks across Europe. Unfortunately that scarcely applies to the Mediterranean; only the lows generated in the northern Adriatic or in the Gulf of Genoa follow a classic track with any frequency. Slow-moving lows are the hardest to assess: even for meteorologists they often enough cause a lot of trouble. Laymen ought not to waste any time on rules for them, let alone speculation.

The depression centre rule

From the shape of the centre of the depression – its innermost isobars – it is often possible to identify its track. If this is distinctly oval, the low's preferred direction of movement will be along the oval's major axis.

The warm sector rule

To remind you: the warm sector is the space between the warm and the cold front. Take a closer look at the isobars in the warm sector: if this is wide open and the isobars then are roughly parallel, the low will move 'along' these. But this rule is only valid for pretty young lows, which are recognizable by the wide warm sector.

Stationary depressions

When a low has reached the last part of its life cycle, it usually becomes either stationary or very slow moving. The recognition key for such lows on the weather map is that their fronts are already substantially occluded. Most don't have a real warm front any more: there only remains a single front line winding in

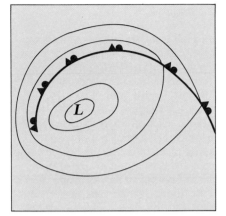

Old, stationary low

A single front makes a wide arc around the depression.

a wide arc around the depression. Such stationary 'old' lows like to assume a guiding role for the new depression systems following them. When the weather buffs talk about a *central low*, an extensive *high-altitude low* or *stationary low*, these all

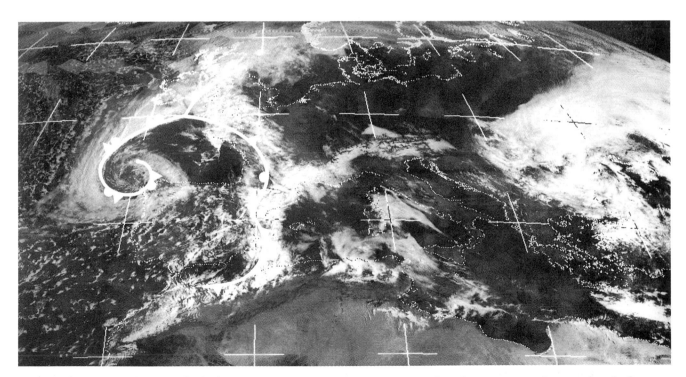

Satellite photo of an occluded depression

A birds-eye view of an aged and fully swirled low. Its centre is near Cape Finisterre in northern Spain; the weather front spirals outwards from this. Over the east coast of Spain the cloud thickens noticeably; *here a new depression is forming which will soon take charge of the weather. White lines indicate the fronts.*

describe the same weather situation. Along its southern flank, the central low steers a succession of small lows quickly from west to east: the weather is changeable. So it is important to know, with this type of weather, whether you are at the southern flank of such a depression or in the middle of it, where the weather is very settled.

Clouds

The structure of the atmosphere

Although the atmosphere has no definite upper boundary, it can be subdivided into layers. Depending on how the question is posed, the number of layers into which it makes sense to divide it varies. For terrestrial weather we distinguish two layers, into which more than 99% of the entire atmospheric mass is concentrated and in which the forces for our weather can be found. That nearest the earth, in which occur all visible phenomena, is called the **troposphere**. The depth of this weather determining layer ranges from 8 to 18 km; above it lies the so-called **stratosphere** which extends out to about 50 km. The zone between these two layers is called the **tropopause**: a term applied analogously to the other layers higher up.

The troposphere

Since all weather events occur here, it is the principal subject of meteorological research. Within it, temperature decreases at a relatively fixed rate with height, and at its upper boundary ranges from $-40°C$ to $-60°C$. Without disrespect for the enormous power of the processes taking place in the weather layer, one must always remain aware of how incredibly thin this is. Consider a globe about 30 cm in diameter: related to this, the thickness – more of a thin-ness! – of the troposphere is 0.2 to 0.5 mm.

In so thin a layer only horizontal currents can really develop on a large scale; nevertheless it is the vertical movements that produce such important phenomena as lows, highs, fronts etc.

The stratosphere

Inside the stratosphere the temperature increases again: at its upper boundary, the **stratopause**, it is once again about the same as at the earth's surface. There are next to no clouds in this layer, the sole exception being the extremely rare mother-of-pearl clouds.

Knowledge about the stratosphere has, I suppose, been spread most effectively via the supersonic planes whose exhaust gases are said to be changing the concentration of ozone in the air, along with the fluorohydrocarbons and chlorofluorocarbons used as propellants in aerosol sprays. It is a fact that the ozone concentration is vital to all life on earth. In the so-called ozone layer (10 to 50 km altitude) a large part of the sun's UV radiation is absorbed: without that ozone we would not be able to enjoy the sun's radiation on earth as we do now, and the earth would be a planet inimical to life.

Cloud types

The cloud pattern in the sky often gives an indication of what is going on in the atmosphere. From the clouds one can judge how stable the air layers are: whether there is a possibility of showers or thunderstorms. The clouds provide information about currents in the troposphere, indicating sudden changes in the weather. If the other weather signs – wind direction and strength, upper wind, barometric trend, and visibility – are taken into account, careful observation of the clouds makes a valid forecast possible.

Clouds and fog/mist are identical – fog and mist are nothing but a cloud resting on the ground. Clouds mostly arise from air being made to rise until cooling causes the moisture in it to condense. Depending on the altitude and the temperature zone of the cloud, it consists of water droplets or ice crystals.

Meteorologists have divided clouds into ten main types, all with various sub-types and hybrids. For our purposes the main types are quite sufficient. We also distinguish between three different cloud levels: high, middle and low. By means of prefixes or suffixes added to the basic cloud names, a cloud can be classified more narrowly, in order to indicate its structure more precisely or to add some other information.

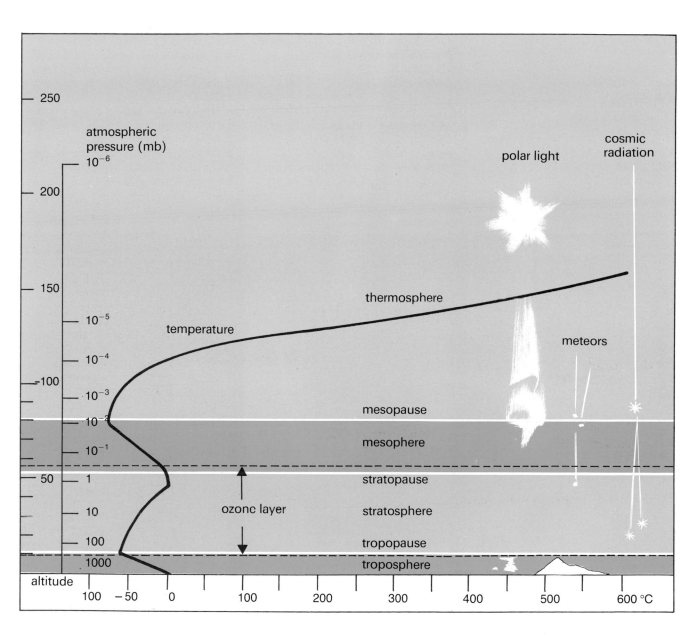

The structure of the earth's atmosphere

The tropopause is the upper boundary of the weather and cloud layer. It lies at an altitude of between 8 and 18 km, depending on season and latitude.

At really high altitudes, the temperature of the air molecules exceeds 1000°C. In spite of that, we could freeze to death, because the density of the air is near zero.

High cloud altitude 6–12 km
Cirrus (Ci)
Cirrocumulus (Cc)
Cirrostratus (Cs)

Middle cloud altitude 2–6 km
Altocumulus (Ac)
Altostratus (As)

Low cloud altitude 0–2 km
Stratocumulus (Sc)
Stratus (St)

Low cloud with vertical development
Nimbostratus (Ns)
Cumulus (Cu)
Cumulonimbus (Cb)

● **Cumulus** are the heaped-up or swelling clouds which occur in all cloud levels.
● **Stratus** are the mostly unstructured, fog-like layer clouds; pretty

shallow but covering a large area.
● **Cirrus** consists of ice-prisms and can therefore only turn up in the top cloud-storey. Also called feather or veil cloud.

High cloud is always called cirrus. Cirrocumulus is a massive, swelling cloud at high level. Altocumulus occurs at middle altitudes, hence the prefix 'alto'. 'Strato' indicates a flattened shape. Altostratus is thus a

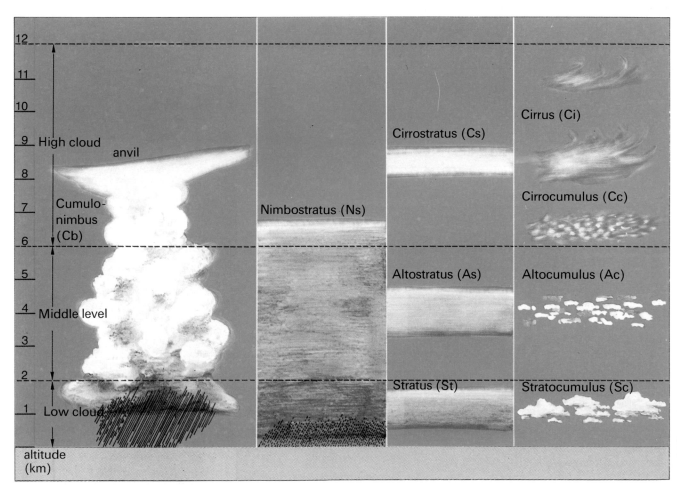

The three cloud levels in the troposphere

46

flat layer cloud at intermediate height.

Unfamiliar designations can be deduced, since the definitions for all combinations are logical: a massive cloud at the bottom level is simply called *cumulus*. When separate cumulus clouds mingle and combine to cover a large area, that cloud is then called *stratocumulus*. If cumulus cloud is found at the intermediate level, it is called *altocumulus*. Really high up, where the jet vapour trails run, that same type of cloud is called *cirrocumulus*. Cumulus extending up into the cirrus level is called *cumulo-nimbus*. The suffix *nimbus* indicates that it brings precipitation.

1

2

Cirrus

1. Separate shreds of cloud like this in the sky are a sign the fine weather will continue.

2. But look out! Meteorologists have a saying 'Women and cirrus are not to be trusted'. The reason is that it is easy to overlook or disregard a gradual concentration of separate elements of cirrus, as shown here, until the whole sky is covered.

3

Cirrus

Cirrus clouds consist of the finest of ice crystals, which is why they have a somewhat soft, fuzzy appearance. They are mostly seen in the summer high-pressure sky and can take a multitude of forms. Entirely contrary to how they appear, they are moving very fast – and are the fastest moving clouds in the sky. It is their great altitude that makes them seem to stand still.

3. Cirrus coming up from the west looking like this should be watched carefully, since it may signal worsening weather. Cirrus coming up from the east and dissolving signals an improvement.

Cirrocumulus

This mostly occurs in large patches and arranged into attractive looking formations such as 'mackerel sky'. Cirrocumulus mostly forms ahead of warm fronts, in the presence of a southerly high-level airstream. It is an indication of increasing humidity in the upper air.

1. If the cirrocumulus is arranged in waves you can count on an early worsening of the weather.

2. Cirrocumulus mostly forms in the presence of a strong southerly high-altitude air-stream; it can also often be seen under föhn *conditions. If the barometer is falling and the cloud comes up from the west, a break-in of cold air is to be expected. The next day will certainly bring bad weather, the warm front in summer frequently showing up only as a band of cloud. The bad-weather zone is linked to the cold front and the inflow of cold air behind it.*

Cirrostratus

The classical harbinger of bad weather, when it comes up slowly like a screen until it finally covers the whole of the sky.

1. After a lengthy period of fine weather one often overlooks the cirrostratus, which initially is still transparent like a hazy covering. First indications of cirrostratus are the halo phenomena. Cirrostratus thickening further, at first still allows the sun through.
2. Later on the cloud cover becomes solid and more cloud comes up underneath it. If at this stage the barometer also starts to fall noticeably, there will be rain soon.

Altocumulus

Very commonly seen, in big fleecy clouds. There is often confusion between cirro- and altocumulus; jet vapour trails, which only form at cirrocumulus level, help to distinguish between the two.

Altocumulus
1. Summer altocumulus, announcing changeable weather. In places, altostratus has already formed. The further development will be progressive thickening of this cloud.
2. Altocumulus arranged in waves or bands is notice of a cold front. Expect showers and thunderstorms.

Altocumulus 3

3. If altocumulus starts to bubble up in lower formations, thunderstorms can be expected within a few hours.

Altostratus 4

A boring type of cloud, which often appears grey shading to blue-grey and in parts is pretty ragged. Thickening altostratus means it will soon rain. Occurs mostly when a front is coming up.

Altostratus

4. If altostratus thickens, as here towards the horizon, there is going to be rain soon. However, if the sun continues to shine through the cloud the weather is not going to get worse. Altostratus following a build-up of cirrus and altocumulus is the classic harbinger of bad weather.

Stratus

The lowest-lying stratus is generally fog or mist. Even when the weather report refers to high fog-type cloud, what is meant is stratus. It is a cloud without structure. Often forms over the sea and along the coast.

Stratus

Shortly after sunset the Spanish coast is being covered by a thick layer of stratus, rolling slowly down to the sea. Just half an hour later and 2 nm out from the coast, we were also shrouded in thick fog, i.e. low stratus.

If stratus comes up in summer, it is going to be muggy and there is a risk of thunderstorms. If below an approaching stratus blanket ragged remains of cumulus are also hanging, there will be rain soon.

Stratocumulus

Sometimes shortened to 'stracu' and the cloud type most widespread in our latitudes. Found at sea under almost all weather conditions. Particularly just after sunrise, it likes to appear as a dense low-hanging covering which usually dissolves rapidly. Stracu which darkens in the evening is not a harbinger of bad weather.

Stratocumulus

1. This type of cloud is the most widespread.
If dense, low-lying 'stracu' forms in the night, there is still no reason to expect bad weather as long as the barometer remains reasonably steady. Provided the blanket breaks up in the morning, the weather will remain fine for the rest of the day.

2. If the barometer is rising and the 'stracu' covering gets denser, as shown here, it will remain cloudy for some days.

Nimbostratus

The classic bad-weather cloud. Prolonged rainfall is associated with this cloud, which belongs to the typical warm front. Nimbostratus is a layer cloud, extending from just above the earth surface to the upper boundary of the troposphere.

Cumulus

There are numerous variants, and a distinction is made between small, medium sized, and large cumuli. It is a type of cloud which usually forms on the spot where it is seen and is an indicator of upward movement of the air, e.g. due to the earth's surface

Cumulus

1. Small and medium-sized cumulus is typically present during spells of fine weather in summer. It has a well defined daily cycle, particularly over land, due to the warming-up of the earth's surface and evaporation of ground moisture.

1

warming up. Its lifetime rarely exceeds an hour.

Small and medium sized cumuli are typical summertime fine-weather clouds. They appear to form out of nothing, once the morning sun has provided some hours' heating; late in the afternoon they dissolve again just as quickly. Often some patches of stracu, developed from the cumuli, are left behind.

A warning of bad weather:
● Cumuli which don't dissolve in the evening;
● Cumuli which are already established in the morning.
● If cumuli are still swelling strongly or towering rapidly by the afternoon, there will be a thunderstorm soon.

Cumulus

2. Medium sized cumulus may look pretty threatening, but in summer it does not bring any precipitation. It is often seen behind cold fronts.
3. If cumulus continues to swell in the afternoon, it needs to be watched to see if it extends up into the ice-forming level. If so, there will be showers and possibly also thunderstorms. This cloud rapidly extended upwards and, accompanied by a line squall, brought a heavy shower.

Cumulonimbus

This mighty cloud is also referred to as Cu-nim. If a cumulus cloud shoots upwards so strongly that its upper boundary region freezes, these parts develop a delicate, fuzzy structure. They may form caps or collars which look like cirrus. Often the ragged-looking upper portion spreads out anvil-fashion: a sign that the cloud has butted against a barrier layer preventing any further movement upwards and thus causing an outward flow. Those whose upper portion starts to fray are in a ripe condition and can bring a thunderstorm. When cumuli turn yellow and their outlines seem to become blurred by a haze, thunderstorms usually follow.

> Showers and thunderstorms come from cumulonimbus. Continuous rain comes from nimbostratus.

Cumulus seen from the air

Although the islands themselves, the Canaries, are barely visible to the naked eye, the accumulation of fine-weather cumulus shows clearly that there are four. Since during the day the islands distinguish themselves from the sea by becoming strongly heated, causing evaporation, they can thus be located by their cloud from a long way off. Flight altitude was 8 km; cirrostratus is visible above the aircraft.

Weather peculiar to coastal regions

The boundary region between shore and sea creates meteorological peculiarities and deviations from the normal weather sequence. This applies to wind as well as cloud cover and the various weather events.

Coast-generated changes

With onshore wind, the basic effect of the coast is to increase the wind speed. Since over land friction produces a retardation of the air mass, the air piles up directly along the line of the coast. As a consequence, the wind speed increases inside a narrow strip parallel to the coast. Swelling cloud is generated directly along the line of the coast. If the weather is already showery, the showers here will get distinctly heavier. There may not be any thunderstorms anywhere else, but

On shore wind

Air flow onto a coast generates a zone lift there, resembling a cold front. The wind changes direction and it increases in strength near land.

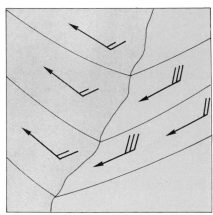

they will then turn up along the coast. With onshore wind you thus get the worst of the weather in the coastal region. The zone of increased weather activity extends about 3–5 nm to seaward and 10–30 nm inland. Particularly in late summer, this type of inflow frequently brings nighttime thunderstorms.

With sideshore wind (blowing along the shore) you get a similar effect. A belt of strong wind is set up parallel to the coast, as a result of bunching of the isobars. The increase in wind strength is especially pronounced if the land rises significantly at the coast or is mountainous.

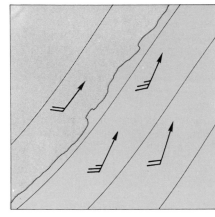

Sideshore wind blowing parallel to the land increases in strength under the coastal edge; the higher that edge, the more the wind speed rises.

Immediately around the coast, 'special' weather develops: more wind, more cloud, more chance of showers or rain than elsewhere, heavier showers than elsewhere, or thunderstorms when the surrounding area just has showers.

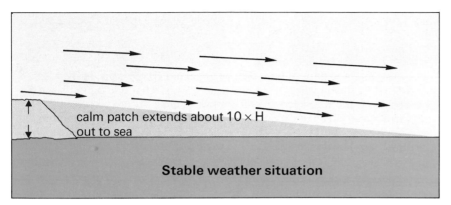

When the weather situation is stable, a calm develops in the lee of the coast.

With offshore wind a zone in which the wind is weak develops parallel to the coast. The higher the coastal contours, the farther out to sea this will extend; roughly speaking, to ten times the height of the coastal ridge. Depending on the predominating weather, one of two phenomena occur in the coastal strip: calm, or wind blowing the other way. When the air mass is stably layered (warm air) there will be a flat calm almost regardless of the prevailing wind strength. When the atmosphere is not stably layered (cold air with cumulus), the wind direction is totally reversed in the coastal strip. The wind blows towards the coast, while a powerful current carries the clouds offshore. This is the result of turbulent eddies standing more or less stably in the lee of the coast. The counterwind is correspondingly gusty. The higher the coastline, the steeper and more pronounced these phenomena.

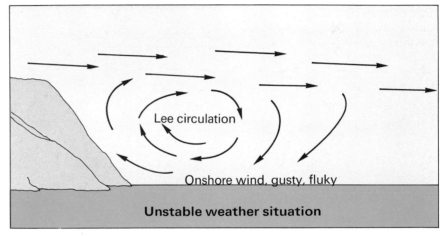

In an unstable weather situation, there is no calm pocket but rather a lee circulation develops, with gusty 'counterwind'.

Locality-based examples
Flensburg Fjord on the Baltic: the inner fjord here can be considered an example for many other fjords and lagoons. With a northwesterly wind, the Danish coast forms a lee. Over a 200–300 m wide strip there is either a flat calm or a good, turbulent, sailing wind in whose gusts those who know the area can gain ground. You can often see two yachts close together running free on opposite headings.

Sardinia and Corsica: with a westerly, summery, sailors's wind there is a flat calm along the east coast of the islands and 5–10 nm to seaward. Anyone just wishing to sail past the islands on the leeward side would do well therefore to give them a wide berth. The same applies with other islands.

On the windward side the conditions already described for onshore wind apply. With islands as high (or coasts as steep) as these, you can easily stay out of the strong-wind zone by going close inshore. The wind there will be substantially less than 1–2 nm out.

59

Corner effects

All pronounced capes can create wind conditions of their own. In particular, very high capes create an unpleasant swirl zone to leeward, if the cape lies across the wind. In the immediate vicinity of a cape there is a substantial strengthening of the wind. Low capes produce less of an unpleasant effect to leeward, but the strengthening of the wind directly at the cape becomes very noticeable. The isobars are here packed together very closely. In strong winds it is a good idea for a yacht to keep several miles farther away from a cape than is required for navigation. This particularly applies to the very steeply rising capes of Corsica and Sardinia.

For example, in a westerly, the wind force at the southern tip of Langeland (Bagenkop) is always raised by at least one figure. Even more acute is the acceleration at Skagen Rev: here the wind strengthens by as much as 2 to 3 forces on the Beaufort scale.

Cape winds

The more prominent and the higher the cape, the more pronounced the circulation to leeward of it. Even small local lows can arise.
1 – flat cape, 2 – steep cape.

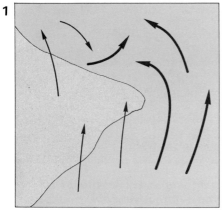

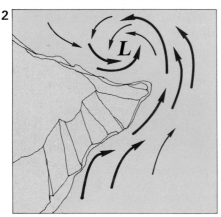

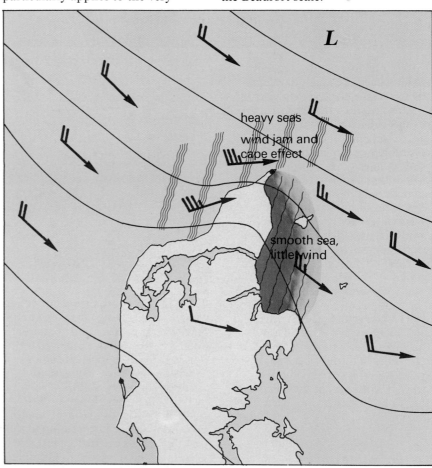

heavy seas
wind jam and cape effect
smooth sea, little wind

Strengthening of wind off Skagen

Anyone wanting to round Skagen coming from the sheltered Kattegat often gets a nasty surprise: the yacht is suddenly buffeted by heavy seas. The wind difference between the Kattegat and open sea can be a full four forces.

Corridor winds

If wind is blowing in through a door or window, it strengthens quite substantially when it finds an outlet to leeward out of the same space; we experience the same effect on a much larger scale in coastal regions. If the wind blows through a narrows, its speed in that region increases. This has several names: funnelling, nozzle effect, corridor effect, etc. Between and approaching two pieces of rising ground, the air is compressed and accelerated; beyond, the wind drops again. Rivers with high banks also channel the wind along them.

Low-lying shores or bays with islands to seaward demonstrate the same wind compression at the narrows. If you want to sail faster here, pick the narrowest passage with the steepest banks. The most unpleasant combination along a coastline is a cape with a 'corridor' beyond it. Here the individual effects multiply

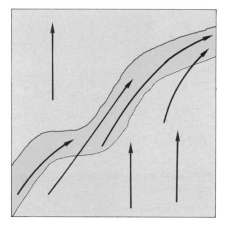

Wind deflection by a river-course

When the principal direction of a river coincides substantially with the wind direction, the latter will follow every bend in the river. Depending on how you're sailing, it will always be from ahead.

one another to such an extent that there can be a full gale blowing in the narrows even when there is a quiet summer breeze everywhere else.

Two well-known examples ocur in the Med. The **Strait of Bonifacio**, between Corsica and Sardinia, with light westerly wind in the open sea is quite enough to produce a full gale, which has already got many people unfamiliar with the region into deep trouble.

The **Straits of Gibraltar** also have driven many a skipper to desperation. It doesn't matter whether it is the prevailing westerly wind you find here or an easterly – until you get to within a few hours of the narrows, the wind blows soothingly evenly and pretty gently. But then it increases steadily, the nearer you get. Anyone having to beat out through must absolutely take the inward flow from the Atlantic and the tidal stream into

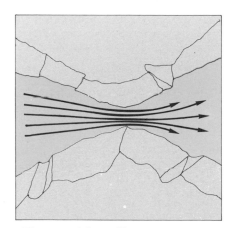

The corridor effect

In the vicinity of a narrows, the wind will always increase, even if there are only relatively low banks on both sides.

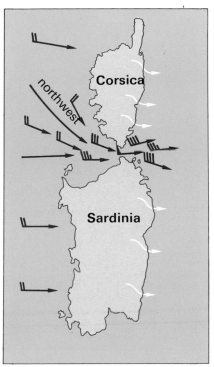

In the Straits of Bonifacio between Corsica and Sardinia, and even a long way east of these, the corridor effect is reinforced by the cape effect, creating a tendency to gale force winds.
White arrows = vertical gusts

Strong wind in the Straits of Gibraltar

When the surface wind is westerly, its strength in the Straits is nearly doubled, this enormous increase being due to the funnel-like convergence of the two coasts. With easterly winds it's only close to Gibraltar that it is unpleasant, but then the seas are steep because the inflow from the Atlantic opposes the wind.

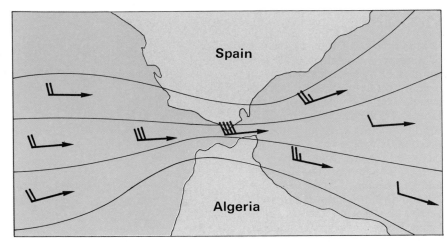

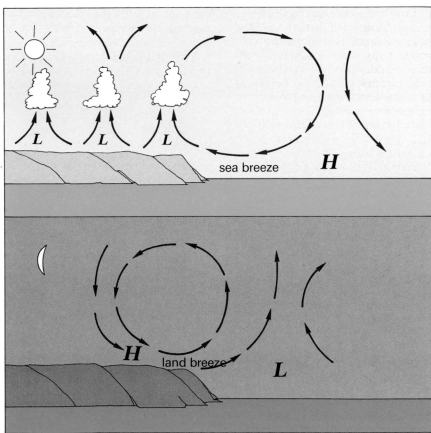

This is how the land sea breeze circulation arises.

account. When there is a decent blow from the west, many a yacht has given up the attempt miserably after a day because it hasn't been able to make good even a single mile to windward. The tides get stronger just to the west, a surprise after the Med.

Land and sea breezes

Air over land warmed on a summer's day rises. From the sea the result of this upward movement is clearly visible as swelling cloud. When making a landfall, you can see such clouds many hours before you can see the land.

The air mass which has risen over the warm land disperses again above the cloud since it can't carry on rising endlessly. It can only flow in the direction where there is too little air and that is back over the sea, because the rising 'land air' draws its replacement in from the sea, thus creating a circulation which is not interrupted until the land is no longer heated sufficiently by the sun.

The circulation

After sunrise there is the usual morning flat calm, then the sea breeze starts up, reaching maximum strength around midday. In the afternoon the wind drops, with dead calm again in the evening. If overnight the land becomes much cooler than the sea, that process is exactly reversed: cloud forms over the sea, clear sky over the land, and a faint land breeze blowing off the shore.

Strength of the sea breeze

Along the North Sea and Baltic coasts, sea breeze strength reaches force 3 to 4 and they extend some 3 to 5 nm out to sea. In the Mediterranean it can get much stronger; e.g. along the east coast of Spain it regularly reaches force 4 to 5, and around Greece it gets even higher (force 6). In the morning it starts between 9 and 11, depending on the locality, dying down again between 5 and 7 pm at the latest. The nocturnal land breeze is distinctly weaker and more variable; along North Sea and Baltic coasts it is a rare occurrence.

Forecast wind strength force 3; actual, force 7 – is there an explanation?
I'm sure it has happened to you often enough that, having been promised a gentle breeze near the coast, you then got a real stinker – or even worse, the opposite, a depressing flat calm. The explanation is the sea breeze, for this gets up independently of the wind to be expected from the lie and spacing of the isobars. So there is nothing special about these two systems operating either in conjunction or in opposition. In opposition, they weaken one another or indeed cancel out altogether in a flat calm. In the other situation you get a really strong wind because the sea breeze has to be added to the larger wind mentioned in the forecast. In the open sea the forecast is accurate enough; only where the sea breeze circulation caused by the land affects it does everything seem upside-down.

Thunderstorms

How do thunderstorms arise?

Many theories have already been put up to explain this complex event, but sadly we are still not in a position to say exactly how a thunderstorm functions.

Thunderstorms are electrical storms, as you learned at school. Only, how come there is anything charged, for nothing can discharge that isn't first charged. The explanation is in the mighty cumulonimbus clouds, essential prerequisites for thunderstorms.

● Thunderstorms are always linked to cumulonimbus.
The body of the earth has an invariable electrical charge, loosely called 'ground' or 'earth' in electricians' jargon. The magnitude of this charge, and whether it is positive or negative, is immaterial in principle; however, the air has an opposite charge. Strong air currents can disturb the air charge, for after all it is the air molecules and the dust and water particles that carry that charge. One of the peculiarities of the thundercloud, which is what cumulonimbus is also called, can be seen from the drawing: updraft and downdraft regions exist in close proximity. The two systems are real 'jetstreams'; the wind speeds in these regions easily exceed 100 km/hr. So here we have the means for a gigantic transport of electrically charged air particles, resulting in a cloud charged like an electrical condenser. Discharges are now possible within this

cloud as well as between it and the earth.

Ground discharges are between cloud and ground; air/cloud discharges are inside the cloud or between cloud portions.

● Thunderclouds form in unstable air masses. There are two causes of air mass instability: strong cooling of the upper layer, and strong heating of the lower.

Instability results in rapid and violent upsetting of the 'falsely positioned' air mass. We see this as heaped-up cloud, so the development of a thunderstorm can be recognized indirectly from the cloud picture. There are two possible ways of ascertaining the danger of thunderstorms:

1. *Observe how the cloud is developing*
● If altocumulus starts towering and acquires ragged edges, that is a sure sign of a rapidly developing thunderstorm. This applies particularly in the Mediterranean.

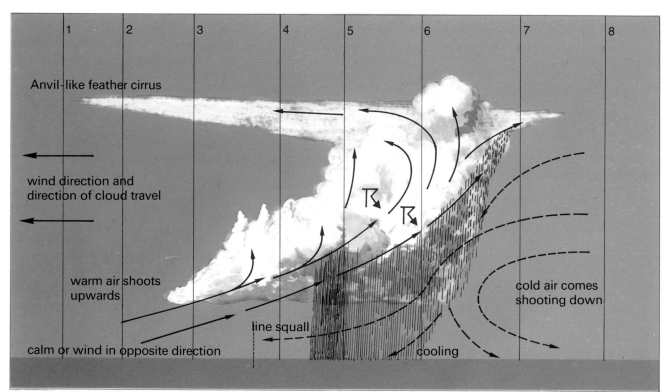

Section through a fully-developed thundercloud (Cumulonimbus)

This is the weather sequence
1. The wind falls calm.
2. A slight, warm wind gets up from the opposite direction.
3. When the thundercloud reaches you, all of a sudden you get a line squall lasting for some minutes.
4. After a short pause, a heavy shower follows, equally suddenly, or hail with thunder and lightning.
5. Change to steady rain.
6. Drastic drop in air temperature.
7. Gusty wind, up to gale force from various directions, at the tail of the thundercloud.
8. Weather calms down.

If cumulus is growing into thundercloud, this is usually observable from the distinct swelling upwards. As long as it continues to swell and the cloud retains its closed, cauliflower-like shape nothing more than a shower can drop from it.

Only when the top part of the cloud undergoes changes is there danger of a thunderstorm starting. You then see 'daughter' clouds in the upper part of the swelling cloud; possibly as a cap floating above the cloud, or level with the top. What is peculiar about these clouds is that they are not of the swelling type, but are feathery like cirrus.

When it has ripened fully, the entire upper part of the thundercloud will have changed. The swellings have been transformed into a diffuse, feathery structure which looks like an anvil. Often, the lower part has simultaneously changed colour to something between yellowish and orange-grey. By no means every cumulonimbus cloud brings a thunderstorm – but it might. It is a question no one can answer in advance for any given case. Electrical discharges occur spontaneously and can only be described in statistical terms.

●If cumulus cloud is swelling powerfully and the upper part is becoming feathery, you must always reckon with thunderstorms.

Thundercloud in the preliminary stage with 'daughter-cloud'. This is feathery and seems to hover above the cumulus. In other places the bulges are becoming frayed. A little later, this became a fully developed thundercloud with an enormous anvil top.

Fully developed thundercloud (cumulonimbus) with classic anvil.
The cloud has butted against the weather layer upper boundary. Further rise is impossible so the air masses must spread out sideways. Temperatures are below −40°C so all water particles are frozen. The anvil is clearly being blown out to the left, which is the direction in which the cloud is travelling.

2. Switch on the radio

Anyone lacking confidence in judging cloud, or unable to see the upper part, should make use of an effect which electrical discharges have on the radio: even when thunderstorms are still a long way off and so there is no thunder, you can already hear an irregular crackling and rattling on medium wave. You still have enough time to take suitable precautions before the storm hits.

If thundercloud is already showing up on the horizon, it is important to know which way it is travelling.
● The direction of travel can be judged from the feathery anvil. Since the cloud is moving with the wind – which, however, is blowing in a very different direction at ground level – the upper part of the cloud is teased-out downwind. The long cirrus tails point in the direction in which the cloud is travelling

Typical weather situation leading to thunderstorms

We distinguish two common types of thunderstorms, both linked to classic weather situations:

● Heat thunderstorms
● Front thunderstorms

Heat thunderstorms arise during periods of fine summer weather, and do so at the western flank of the high-pressure area. On this side warm and moist subtropical air from

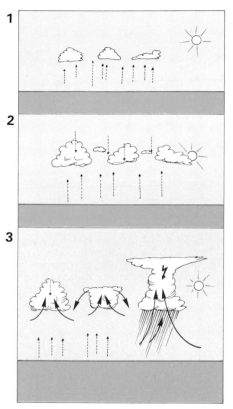

1

2

3

How heat thunderstorms
develop in the course of the
day.
1. morning, 2. midday,
3. afternoon and evening

**Thunderstorm-bearing
northerlies**

*This is a typical weather situa-
tion favouring summer thunderstorms. Cold air extending
high up advances over the
warm water and triggers thunderstorms. A cold front
approaching after a period of
high pressure, high temperature and high humidity
weather always threatens
thunderstorms.*

the Mediterranean area flows northwards. Since this process takes place
preferably at the lower levels, the air
layering becomes unstable, particularly in the late afternoon when the
sun's warmth is no longer so strong
and the upper layer of air is already
starting to cool off again. That is
typical for heat thunderstorms over
land; over the sea the reaction of the
air is much slower because the water
surface does not have any significant
daily temperature cycle. Therefore,
heat thunderstorms arise in the
second half of the night, if at all.

Front thunderstorms are almost
exclusively linked to cold fronts.
Whenever a cold front is suddenly
due to pass through after several
days of fine weather, you have to
count on heavy thunderstorms
around the front and also behind it.
These are substantially heavier than
the mostly harmless heat thunderstorms.

Tactics in thun-
derstorms

As thunderstorms can bring serious
danger, it is important to know what
these are and to act appropriately.
Depending on the type of boat and
the specific situation, it may be one
or another of the following which
brings the danger:
● Wind shift by up to 180°
● Sudden, strong temperature drop
● Lightning strike
● Extremely poor visibility
● Rough sea
● Hail
● Strong wind gusts

 In many situations, if a thunderstorm threatens the best advice is
either to go into a harbour or to find
a safe anchorage. In a true cold front
thunderstorm, the gusts can be up to
hurricane strength, particularly over
warm water – so, down all sails, lash

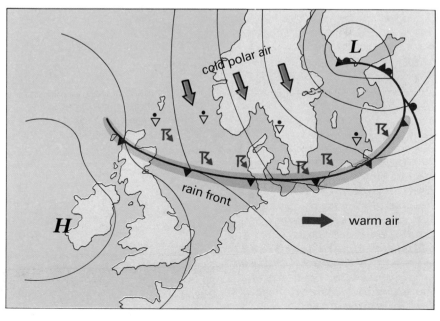

everything securely and look for cover. The direct life-threatening danger is lightning. No-one can side-step a lightning strike, far less forecast when or where it will hit. The insidious thing about lightning is its unpredictability; not even the lightning itself 'knows' what it is going to do in the next second. All the time it is looking in a new direction for a suitable target, and only when it is a mere 10 m short of this does it 'acknowledge' it and strike. As a rule it is an upstanding object which conducts electricity well and has good contact with the earth.

Waterspouts

Waterspouts are exactly the same as whirlwinds: the former expend themselves over the sea, the latter over land. Both could be called mini-tornados. For a waterspout to arise two conditions have to be fulfilled:

1. the water must be noticeably warmer than the air.
2. there must be a thundercloud (cumulonimbus).

When there is a current of polar air over the sea behind a cold front,

Waterspout

1. Coming out from the underside of a cumulonimbus cloud, the trunk extends rapidly downwards. Clearly recognisable, the 'stalactite' hanging from the cloud base creates the potential (here realised) for a waterspout to form. The trunk swirls the water upwards and from this mini-tornado obtains further nourishment.

2. The fully developed water-spout. Towards the right in the picture there is heavy rain. In the background, more vigorous swelling clouds.

3. The maturity and final stage. The trunk keeps on getting longer and thinner, while developing a number of bends, until it finally tears and the waterspout disintegrates.

both conditions are generally fulfilled. The cold air warms up in the proximity of the sea surface, and in the process absorbs a lot of evaporated moisture. This brings the atmosphere into an unstable condition, because the polar air (cold up to a considerable height) is warmed excessively from underneath and that bottom layer wants to rise. If above that rising air there is a large thundercloud, that upward flow is reinforced powerfully, for the cloud sucks up that warm, moist air. Now, if in the atmosphere there is something going up, somewhere else there must be something coming down – which is precisely where a waterspout can arise.

If you have ever studied a thundercloud carefully, you will know that there are often udder-like protuberances from the underside (called 'mamma' in technical language). These downpointing bulges are caused by downdrafts shooting out of the cloud. If the air between the sea and the cloud is very unstable, one of these many bulges can suddenly extend downwards. While it is descending like a viscous droplet, coincidentally nearby some of the warm and moist air goes shooting up into the cloud from underneath. This generates a fast-moving swirling action, which rapidly converts the drop into a downward-pointing trunk. While this grey trunk is winding its way downwards it seems to swing to and fro searchingly in order to suck up anything nearby. The warmed, moist air is full of energy which strengthens this minor eddy second by second; its diameter grows all the time and it keeps extending downwards.

So far, all you can see of the waterspout is a trunk swinging to and fro. Suddenly spray is swirled up from the water surface without the grey funnel reaching down to it. The waterspout is complete and carries on growing. The bottom part of the trunk is invisible: only when it extends down so far that the swirling air sucks water upwards with enormous force does the waterspout show up at surface level. Spray is flung up in a funnel shape, the trunk helps itself generously to warm water in the process and draws it up into the cloud. Wind speeds inside the trunk of a waterspout can exceed 150 knots – well beyond the Beaufort scale. The air in the trunk can rotate either way.

One of the dangers connected with a waterspout, of course, arises from the incredibly high wind speeds, which leave scarcely anything undamaged. But even greater damage is done by the sudden partial vacuum created if a waterspout passes over the top of a boat. The atmospheric pressure in the centre of the trunk is about as low as that in a hurricane. Unfortunately there are next to no atmospheric pressure measurements for waterspouts: none of the instruments have stood the test. Pressure in the centre is so low that everything seems to burst when the trunk passes over it. So be very careful not to have the honour of having a waterspout on board: neither craft nor crew would have much chance of surviving the experience.

Tactics around a waterspout
It is entirely possible to be surprised by a sudden waterspout if sailing under a thundercloud – after all, these horrors are chance occurrences and give no warning. Since the spout derives from a thundercloud and remains tied to it, it also keeps moving with it. So one can escape most easily by steering at right angles to the direction of cloud travel if the trunk gets dangerously close. But take care! Don't forget that thunderclouds don't move in the direction of the ground-level wind: keep your eye on the clouds, because they are travelling with the high-level wind.

The sea's motion: tidal and ocean currents

What actually is 'the sea's motion'?
It is the combination of sea and swell. **Swell** is an old, running-down sea whose driving force is no longer effective: an aged sea. **Sea** is the current, wind-generated, wave condition of the water. 'The sea's motion' thus always designates the overall state of the water surface and takes into account earlier wind effects. Only a synopsis of the effects of both earlier and present winds gives us full information about the actual motion of the sea in a given area.

Ground swell is a wave whose trough extends down nearly to the sea-bottom. It arises when a long, high swell reaches shallow water.

Groundswell over shallow water

The ground swell shown here is significantly more dangerous than heavy seas in a gale, because the wave trough – and thus the vessel's keel – reaches down to the sea-bottom. Due to its high speed of travel (20 to 30 kn) and its exceeding steepness, such a wave will capsize vessels or break them up by grounding.

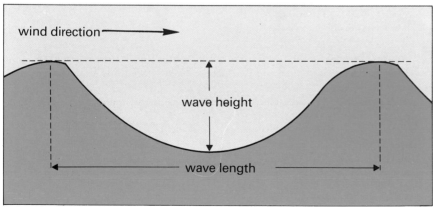

Definitions relating to the sea's motion

Wave length is the distance from crest to crest; wave height the height-difference between trough and crest. The period is the time interval between the passage of successive wave crests. The wave slope facing the wind is noticeably longer than that away from it. Sailing into the wind means running into the steeper wave front.

Cross-seas comprise two separate seas coming from different directions, producing a composite wave pattern. Cross-seas often arise when a cold front is passing rapidly: ahead of the front, sea from SW was set up; once the front has passed and the wind swings around to NW to N, the two seas are running in conflict. Admittedly the older sea decays to swell, but there are still two seas coming from different directions, whose waves are superimposed. The resulting waves are particularly feared since they are irregularly spaced and at the same time can reach extreme heights with deep troughs.

Any expanse of water that does not have deep-sea characteristics will demonstrate variations in the wave structure co-determined by factors other than the weather. The following factors influence the water motion in a given region:

- Wind strength
- Wind fetch and duration
- Depth of water and its variation
- Current and/or tidal streams

When does a wave break?
The normal wave gradient is about
1 in 7, i.e. if a wave is 1 m high it will
be about 7 m long. For that to apply,
the depth of water must be at least
three times the wave length, otherwise this ratio will be reduced and
the wave will get steeper. The shallower the depth, the steeper the wave
will get until finally it breaks. When
the depth of water is less than half
the wave length, there will certainly
be breakers. Some will form already
when the two are about the same.

   From this it follows that swell
getting into shallow water is particularly dangerous. Swell waves are very
long; for example, way out in the
German Bight the depth of water is
substantially less than the length of
the swell wave. The result is very
heavy breakers on the coast and in
the sea near the coast.

The effect of fetch

Obviously, waves do not immediately conform to the strength of the
wind. When a wind gets up, the
waves will build up gradually and it
will be some time before the sea has
risen to correspond, the reason for
this being the inertia of the water.
The farther the distance over which a
wind blows, the greater the 'fetch'.
When a wind increases after a day of
flat calm, to a force 4 wind for

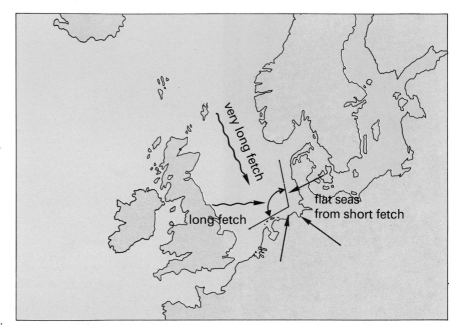

Fetch in the North Sea

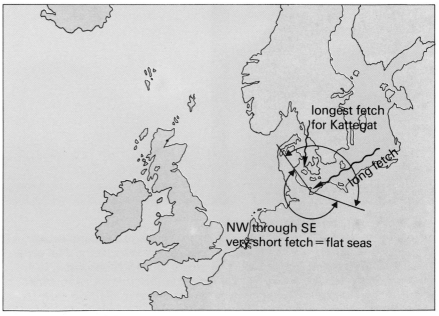

Fetch in the Baltic

instance, it will take one to two hours for the sea to develop fully. When thunderstorms or showers with hefty gusts reaching gale force pass, you rarely get a rough sea because the effective duration of the strong wind is too short, and usually it also changes direction. The sea merely becomes choppy and calms down again quickly in the wake of this bad weather. The following descriptions assume that the wind has been at a given strength for long enough to have produced the corresponding wave height. Another significant factor is, the distance which the wind has been effective over the sea.

North Sea

The unfavourable wind directions here, as regards fetch, are from west to north. Wind from those directions can apply itself to the water over many hundreds of miles; correspondingly this is where you get the highest waves. From the northwest a swell can carry on running for up to three days after the gale has long gone.

Winds from between south and east bring the most agreeable seas for the coast of continental Europe, the reason being the short working-up distance for the wind to take effect. Only far out at sea and near the Eastern shores of the U.K. does the motion build up to correspond to the wind strength.

Baltic

This is the opposite to the North Sea when it comes to fetch. Westerly to northwesterly winds cause the least motion; the protection provided by Denmark prevents any major sea buildup. That doesn't apply to the central and eastern Baltic; no farther out than Rügen the westerly wind starts to build up a pretty fierce sea. Northerly as well as southerly winds produce an agreeably smooth sea in the western Baltic. However that is not so in the Belts and the Sound, where a rough sea gets up very quickly, particularly with southerly winds. As a result of channelling in the narrow, long passages between the islands, the wind strengthens by one or two forces and pushes the Baltic water into the Belts. High and uncomfortably steep waves result. Consistent with the long fetch, easterly winds build up the highest waves. Fortunately a long-lasting swell, as in the North Sea, does not

arise in the Baltic: the water is too shallow.

Water depth and the sea's motion

A wave which arrives in shallower water is slowed down by friction against the sea-bed. The more rapidly the water shallows, the greater that braking effect at the bottom. In other words, the lower part of the wave is held back and thus moves more slowly. The upper part which we can see is braked scarcely or not at all. That makes the wave shorter and steeper: its upper part is moving faster than the lower, eventually overtaking it and steepening until it breaks.

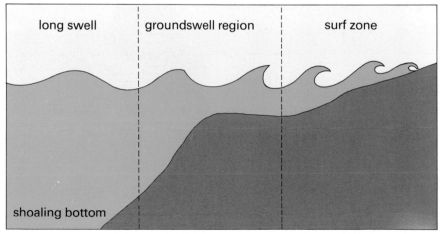

How the sea's motion develops when the waves come to shallow water.

Shallow water – flat seas

Great Belt, force 7–8 wind. Because it is so shallow, the waves can't reach any great height; even at only 1 m they start to break. A wicked sea for small boats because they sheer and/or may broach-to.

Anyone out in a boat in a choppy sea should look out for shallows when setting his course. The seas there get as steep and rough as if the wind were two or three forces higher.

Deeper water – higher seas

East coast of Spain, force 8, wave height some 3 to 4 m with 70 m depth of water. Many breakers, because the sea comes from a water depth of 1000 m.

The sensible thing is to avoid those areas; both craft and crew will be thankful, since the steepness of waves over these shallows creates trouble. The hull crashes down hard, and only slowing down significantly or turning away from the wind reduces the stress. In strong winds, to say nothing of gale conditions, one should absolutely avoid sailing over such patches. Deflection around islands or shallow areas can also cause dangerous rough, confused seas on the leeward side, even in deeper water.

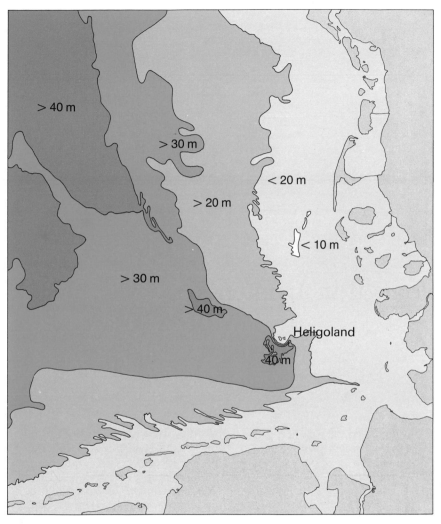

Map of the Southern North Sea with lines of constant depth

3 nm, you will find a relatively calm sea outside. In the Great Belt, southerly winds also make for rough seas.

The influence of tides and currents on waves

Currents (horizontal water flow) and tidal streams exert considerable influence on waves. The stronger the currents, the more they modify the wave situation. There are two extreme cases with which we have to live in tidal waters:

1. wind and tidal stream going the same way.
2. wind and tidal stream in opposition.

When wind and tide direction are the same, a noticeable smoothing-out of the waves results. The sea behaves as though there were scarcely any wind. When tide and wind are in opposition, the sea becomes short and steep. The waves then break even when there is relatively little wind, producing a pretty uncomfortable ride and a noticeable slowing-down.

If I have to decide when best to leave harbour, one of the things I always take into account is the relationship between wind and tide. In any strong wind, I prefer to face a sea that is smoothed by wind and tide, even if I lose out in distance made good because of unfavourable drift. Tide behind you with the wind against makes things more laborious than running against the tide (with engine assistance) in a relatively smooth sea.

North Sea

Here it's all narrow inlets. Particularly dangerous are the approaches to Norderney (even at high water), to the River Jade via the middle channel, and to Amrum and Sylt via the Amrum Bank and the Vortrapp Deep. Heligoland is similarly tricky, shortly before you get there.

Baltic

When the wind is strong from the east, Schleimünde has a steep sea at the mouth of the entrance channel. If you can get through the first 2 to

Wave heights and lengths during gales				
Sea area	*Wave height*	*Length*	*Speed*	*Maximum height*
W. Baltic	3 m	50–70 m	15–20 kt	6–8 m
North Sea,				
southern	6 m	120 m	20 kt	8–10 m
northern	8–9 m	180–200 m	30–35 kt	10–15 m
N. Atlantic	16–18 m	250 m	30–35 kt	about 30 m

On-board meteorological instruments

Sudden weather changes are potentially dangerous and something you should be prepared for in good time. How do you avoid being surprised by a sudden development? Most emphatically, I want to warn against attaching too much value to the interpretation of cloud. It takes an expert to interpret the ever-changing cloud picture correctly. Mostly the sky is useful for short-term forecasting. Few visible phenomena are reliable harbingers of changes in the weather; anyone sighting worsening weather in the offing is usually already to close to it. The only alternative comes from meteorological instruments which can measure physical quantities relating to the atmosphere and the weather. The range of instruments on the market is vast, and the question becomes then 'which instruments for my boat?'.

Barometers

The only meteorological quantity which really can be measured on board without any disturbing influence from the environment is the atmospheric pressure. Fortunately nature has arranged that it is one of the indicators which will help us to understand present and coming weather. However, I repeat: it is not the absolute value of atmospheric pressure that is decisive, but the measure of its change. Anyone with a decent barometer on board will notice if an official bulletin is suspect especially if he has a basic knowledge of the weather and observes its individual elements carefully and correctly. Unfortunately. I have rarely found a yacht that had a really serviceable barometere fitted. Inevitably you find prettily designed, highly polished, brass ones. And is such a nice-looking barometer adequate? No, because all you have bought is a cheap (or not so cheap) nautical looking room barometer, a long way off being a *real* instrument.

When is a barometer fit for on-board use? Briefly, if it is constructed robustly, and is sufficiently sensitive, to measure atmospheric pressure with the utmost precision. It should remain totally unaffected by the harsh conditions on board. A yacht is an extremely 'barometrophobe' environment with permanent high humidity, continuously changing air temperature, heavy vibration and blows to the hull – all transmitted to the barometer. Stresses like that can only be withstood if an instrument has been specially made for the purpose.

Regarding barometer precision:

for the usual range of atmospheric pressures, lying between 980 and 1030, it must be able to measure changes of less than 1 hPa to be any use – but that means measurement accuracy better than 1 per thousand. Try asking a technician how much one would have to pay for an electrical instrument of that quality.

The high price of a good sea-going barometer, is fully justified. The cells of the measuring unit are carefully artificially aged in a climatic chamber to prevent any contraction or expansion of the wall material affecting the measurements. A cheap barometer, on the other hand, ages naturally: it

won't start functioning without that sort of error until you're too old to go sailing any more. If one fine day the pointer of one of these cheap barometers barely moves, it may not be on account of the weather. You may assume that either the precision engineering has given up the ghost or one of the vacuum cells has developed a leak. Lastly there is the possibility, often experienced, that the whole apparatus has simply rusted up inside.

But more dangerous still are the unnoticed minor errors, which can add up at random. The cheap individual parts of most cheap barometers can start living an active life of their own, resulting in random errors in the pointer reading. A skipper who lacks a proper basis for comparison will never discover the secret life of his barometer. On board my training yacht *Jule* there is one of these cheaper nautical looking barometers in every compartment. A comparison with the precision barometer in the saloon is part of our instrument training. The cheap barometers lead a life of their own, each in its own way. When the precision barometer shows a pressure rise of 3 mb over the past hour, the brass barometer is gaily carrying on falling as though the front were still approaching. Another one first stopped at some point and is now very gradually getting better. These cheap instruments may lag behind the true atmospheric pressure by up to eight hours.

Some readers will object, that after all they are more concerned with the trend of the pressure than with its true value: I trust you will already have noted the fallacy of this deduction when that argument, though basically correct, is applied to the barometer. After all, the pressure changes are about a thousand times smaller than the atmospheric pressure itself – and it is precisely in this order of magnitude that we must work. A cheap barometer has a measurement accuracy of about ± 4–5 mb – totally useless for measuring a pressure change of the order of 1–3 mb.

Another example: the shipping bulletin mentions a small depression moving rapidly eastwards; core pressure 1005, deepening. You tap your barometer and are quite content to get a reading of 1016, thus believing yourself to be a long way from the centre. No need to worry, you announce: the wind has even dropped. In the course of the forenoon the pressure carries on falling steadily, but it's still 1013. Since the wind is still light, you fear no evil. The low must have travelled otherwise than anticipated – after all, your barometer proves that.

But, when last did you calibrate it? It may easily read 6 hPa too high, because the winter lay-up hasn't done it any good and maybe it has never been calibrated. That would make the present situation rather interesting, because the depression is already close to the boat where a properly calibrated instrument would read not 1013 but the actual 1007.

False readings lead to false assessment of the weather situation. Anyone with safety at heart can't sail without a good on-board barometer; it's part of the obligatory equipment for a seagoing boat. Only a few manufacturers produce instruments capable of meeting the requirements of seagoing yachts. On board our *Jule*, I have for some years been using a precision barometer, which has accompanied me over 9,000 miles and through many heavy gales and other adversities without ever failing. It's worth every penny!

Barographs

Anyone wanting to have a really good understanding of the pressure situation buys a **barograph** that continuously records the actual atmospheric pressure. Once you've worked with one of these instruments, you wouldn't be without it. The continuous development is strikingly recorded, so that at a glance you get a clear picture. Any front passing shows up nicely. A big advantage of a written record is that you can read off the pressure changes for preceding hours: there are no lost values. That is very important on board, because when the weather is behaving critically there is little time to keep on tapping the barometer and recording the reading.

However, a barograph is relatively expensive. There are cheap ones available but I advise against acquiring one since they are of unknown foreign manufacture, lacking any parts-supply organization and without guarantee/maintenance service. I know of some instruments for which the seller can't even provide spare paper charts.

Ordinary barographs have a measuring unit comprising two to four cells, connected in series to increase sensitivity and improve accuracy. For the particularly heavily stressed on-board barographs, reputable manufacturers connect up seven to nine cells. To prevent the craft's motion being transmitted to the recording, the recorder casing is mounted on antivibration pads and the pointer is fitted with an oil dashpot. The additional costs for a really seaworthy barograph will show up the first time you get a lumpy sea. Ordinary barograph pointers jump all over the whole

The barograph records atmospheric pressure on a paper-covered drum, which allows you at any time to build up a picture of the way the weather is developing, provided you either have evaluated the shipping bulletin carefully or carry weather facsimile.

scale, covering it in smears: you could scarely get a more impressive comparison between a good and a poor instrument.

A good barograph is distinguished by especial compactness. It can be mounted on a shelf or on a free-standing console and still withstand any gale, thanks to the mounting bolt supplied. The cover is thick Plexiglass so that the instrument is not only well protected but also can be read easily from every direction. Long gone is the day of inky blots: it used to be rather a bore when the good ink for the recording arm was found all over the boat. Now we use cartridge pens which last for a whole season and are easy to change. One paper chart per week is clamped onto the recorder drum, and the drum wound once a week. Do stick with the old windable drums: they are indestructible. An electric drum feeder is an imaginary luxury: batteries and motors are a lot more trouble than gears and springs. You get such a feeling if idiotic help-lessness when the barograph stops recording because the last battery has been exhausted.

1. The quality of recording from a good on-board barograph, when the yacht is being tossed about in a gale.

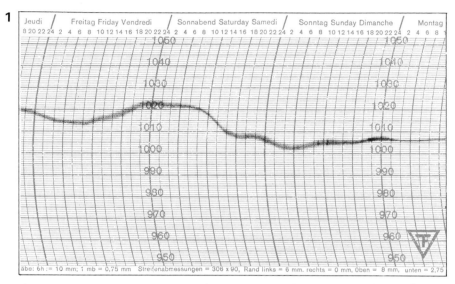

2. And that is what you get from a cheap instrument. Not a lot of use for taking a reading.

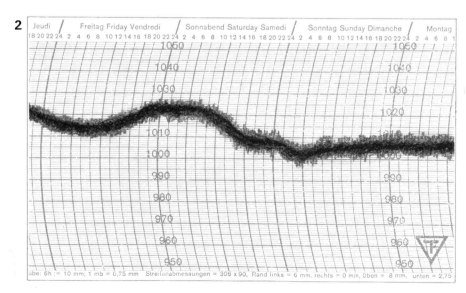

Anemometers

Even for cruising yachts, an anemometer is useful. Particularly if you consider that it's not everyone who has the gift of estimating wind strength from the sea state.

Unfortunately the wind has the unattractive characteristic of varying in strength with altitude. At the surface of the sea, the wind speed is precisely zero; higher up, it increases in accordance with a complicated logarithmic law. The wind corresponding to the isobars only occurs from about a thousand metres upwards. The explanation for this peculiar behaviour lies in the friction between the air and the earth, or rather the surface of the water, producing loss of energy in the form of velocity. The further we remove our anemometer from the water surface the less the influence of this friction becomes and the greater

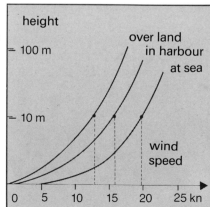

How the wind increases with height.

therefore the wind speed. If we want to measure representative, i.e. comparable, values we must mount the anemometer at a standard height. The weather services worldwide have agreed on a height of 10 m. Now that cannot be achieved on every yacht, so remember that you will measure a high or a low value of wind speed depending on whether your anemometer is mounted higher or lower.

Practical advice on locating the sensor

The masthead is without doubt the most suitable place, but remember that the sensor should not be mounted beside, in front of, or behind the radar reflector, which disturbs the air flow to such an extent that you measure everything bar the true velocity. Therefore install the sensor on a forward-pointing arm from the masthead. Motor yachts often have it mounted directly on the cabin roof, not a good solution. Do mount the revolving cups at least on top of the mast, however short that may be. The farther the sensor is from the bulk of the craft, the better.

Using hand-held anemometers

These are just as reliable and accurate as their fixed brethren but there is one thing to watch: never measure in the cockpit as that's bound to produce a nonsense. Stand to windward and stretch your arms upwards and outwards to get the anemometer as far away from the boat as possible.

Another piece of advice: remember that anemometers always measure the *apparent wind* which may be very different from the true wind. Run-

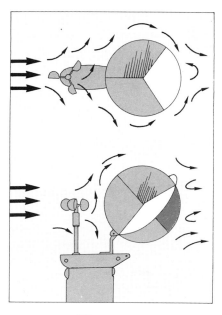

Disturbance of air flow by the radar reflector

The reflector alters the way the air flows so as to generate a large turbulent zone. This zone can be so unfortunately located that the anemometer does not rotate even in a gale. (seen from above and from the side)

ning downwind, add the boat's speed to the indicated value to get approximately the true wind speed. Close to the wind – or going directly into it under engine – you correspondingly subtract the boat's speed (water speed ± tide) from the measured wind speed. On all other courses lying between those two, I always interpolate.

Hand-held anemometer

Hold the instrument as far and as high as possible to windward. Observe the float of the pointer. The wind is continually rising and dropping, and this gustiness is an important factor. At maximum deflection, press the locking button so that you can take the reading at leisure in the cockpit.

Beaufort Wind Scale			
No.	General Description	Mean Velocity (knots)	Sea Criteria
0	Calm	Less than 1	Sea like a mirror
1	Light Air	1–3	Ripples: no foam crests in open sea
2	Light Breeze	4–6	Small wavelets: glasslike crests that do not break
3	Gentle Breeze	7–10	Large wavelets: Crests begin to break: some white horses
4	Moderate Breeze	11–16	Small longer waves: white horses
5	Fresh Breeze	17–21	Moderate waves: many white horses: some spray
6	Strong Breeze	22–27	Large waves: white foam crests: spray
7	Near Gale	28–33	Sea heaps up: white foam blown in streaks
8	Gale	34–40	Moderately high waves: some spindrift: well marked foam streaks.
9	Strong Gale	41–47	High waves: crests begin to topple and tumble: spray affects visibility.
10	Storm	48–55	Very high waves: sea surface becomes almost white: sea tumbles violently
11	Violent Storm	56–63	Exceptionally high waves: sea covered in foam: visibility badly affected.
12	Hurricane	64 +	Air filled with foam & spray: sea white: visibility seriously affected.

The shipping forecast

The list of possible sources of information for weather reports is longer than is generally believed. But which sources offer the better, or even the best, information for a skipper? All reports stem from the same source, if not even from the same met office: why then do they vary so much? When considering this question, one must always bear in mind that each special report and forecast is aimed at a particular audience.

Local station radio broadcasts are for the information of the general populace. If possible, avoid using that forecast as a basis for cruise planning. 'Fair to cloudy with local showers' or 'gentle to moderate breeze during the day, stronger gusts at times along the coast' is no use to those engaged in aquatic sports. Some yachting reports are not much better, mostly limited to a statement about wind strength and direction –

and even that pretty broadly, for the whole day and the whole area.

The shipping bulletins from the coastal radio stations are the best available source of information: you should under no circumstances start out without up to date information. Whether that source by itself is sufficient depends on the sea region involved.

Information density in weather broadcasts is high – too high for many listeners. Try testing yourself using the following text, to see whether after reading it through quickly once (then cover it up, and don't cheat!) you have grasped the entire content of this report:

On the eastern flank of a high moving slowly southwards, strengthening further meanwhile and transferring its

A weather report and the 11 pieces of information it contains

'Along the eastern flank (1) of a high (2) moving slowly (3) southwards (4), strengthening the while (5) and transferring its centre of gravity (6) to the western Mediterranean (7), there is a transient (8) inflow of cool sea air (9) which will slowly come to a stop in the course of the day (10) and which brings a temporary stabilisation of the weather (11) in the forecast area.'

centre to the western Mediterranean, there is a transient inflow of cool sea air which will come to rest slowly in the course of the day and will temporarily quieten the weather in the forecast area.

This everyday but confusing text contains eleven pieces of important information about the weather situation – would you have known that?

Here are the most important findings and deductions from that typical text:

1. If cool sea air is flowing in towards Germany on the eastern flank of the high, the centre of the high must be over the British Isles.
2. The centre of the high is said to be moving slowly southwards, towards the Mediterranean Sea.
3. Pressure at the centre of the high is said to be increasing further, so for the Med one could count on settled weather.
4. For the North Sea and the Baltic, the movement of the high's centre means backing winds (from northwesterly to westerly and southwesterly).
5. With the backing winds it's going to get warmer, but visibility is going to worsen.
6. In early summer, there is a risk of fog if the air is warmer than the sea.
7. With the high moving away, the North Sea and Baltic weather is going to beome unsettled because it will be determined by passing depression zones. (See earlier chapter on typical European weather situations.)

The majority of seagoing yachts are equipped with at least a medium wave radio receiver. For times when transmission comes too early, I recommend a small 12 V timeswitch

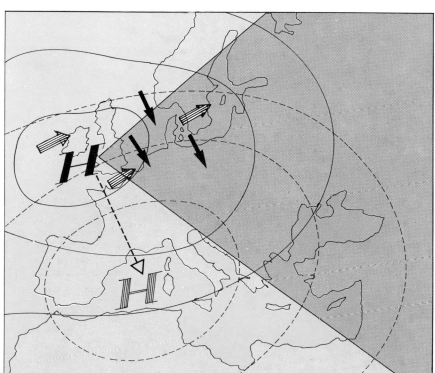

together with a cassette recorder.

Whether you listen to a coastal radio station or the broadcast shipping forecast, don't just limit yourself to listening to the early morning services, even in the best of weather. All forecasting involves uncertainty to a greater or lesser degree; instead of 'forecasting', it would be better to say 'prediction' or even 'advice'. The inference of absolute correctness attached to the word 'forecast' all too often leads to the mistake of listening to just one broadcast and relying blindly on what it says. Even the very best weather advice must be checked against the reality. Anyone who takes a bit of trouble in making his own weather observations is armed pretty well against incorrect forecasts and their disagreeable consequences.

The regional radio service on VHF

The regional maritime radio service is one with which my experience has been good. This service is for a designated region and is transmitted on VHF maritime radio frequencies (not receivable with ordinary VHF radios). In the German Bight coastal region it's better to listen to the working frequencies of the regional centres than on Channel 16. The reports from the centres contain useful information about ship movements, navigational warnings, and above all up-to-date reports on the weather in the region. Wind and visibility prognoses are broadcast as well as warnings of short-notice weather deterioration. British and Continental Services are listed in the nautical almanacs, with the languages used. Quite a few are in English.

Strong wind and gale warnings

Many a cruising sage will claim that such warnings usually arrive when it has already been blowing for half a day or else the warning goes out for days when the air is barely stirring. Well, there is a lot of truth in this. All too often the warning reaches the skipper too late – and only timely warnings have any value. After all, it's little use the duty met man recognizing the situation in time if the warning isn't broadcast until hours later.

In this connection it is necessary to explain the principle behind such a 'warning'. Much of the criticism is groundless, because the skippers' basic assumptions differ from the weathermen's: the meteorologist always warns of the *danger* of strong wind or gales. This in no way means that this *must* occur, merely that the occurrence of strong winds cannot be ruled out, or is possible, or even probable – so a warning of this danger is issued. Of course quite often that danger does not materialize. A wind *warning* is thus basically different from a *prediction*. The prediction (forecast) embodies the most likely of all possible developments; the warning merely the risk of a deviation therefrom. For skippers, warnings therefore are a further decision-making aid in combination with weather advice and his own indispensable observations.

Weather bulletins in foreign waters

It's all very well for anyone who knows a foreign language to recommend listening to a foreign weather report rather than one's own. How many times have you heard a club-chum say that he prefers some other service because it's much more comprehensive, compressed, etc. Whoever sails in foreign waters ought to use the local weather broadcasts if he is at all capable of interpreting the language, simply because experience indicates that every met man is most at home on his own ground. The greater the distance between the area being advised on and the office doing the advising, the less the met man knows about it and naturally the more unreliable his forecast.

Foreign language weather terms are found in almanacs, and a short list is in the back of this book. Learning enough doesn't take as much practice as one might think, because the score or so of words that form the essential part of a weather report turn up again and again. If you record foreign weather reports on tape you will learn those scraps of language particularly quickly. Some Continental services also broadcast in English: anyone sailing from German shores towards England should not tie himself into knots trying to receive Norddeich Radio for as long as possible, but rather should change over to Dutch weather reports which are also transmitted in English. Anyone in the Baltic drawn towards Gotland will find that the English language weather reports of the Poles and the USSR offer something better than Kiel Radio with clearer reception.

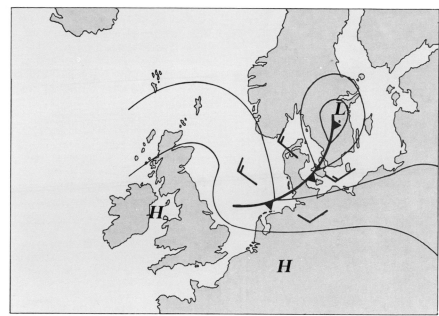

Shallow depression with slow-moving cold front

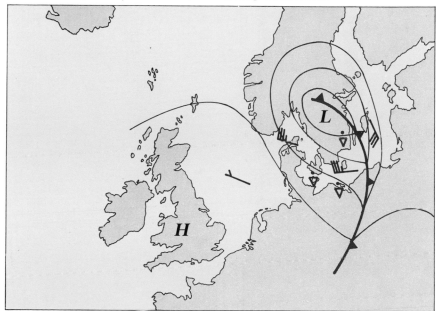

Shallow depression with fast-moving cold front brings a situation totally different from that of a slow-moving front.

Now and then it happens that two different weather services issue differing or indeed highly contradictory forecasts. How can that happen? After all, all met men are trained pretty much the same way, at least in Europe; all work with the same natural physics of the atmosphere – and none has a special line to God!

Leave aside all the cases where one station forecasts SW4 and the other 'southerly winds 4 to 5'. That just conceals assessment margins, experience, pattern of the day, etc. Let us look at the really pronounced differences, which often leave those afloat totally confused. If, for instance, a cold front reaches the Western Approaches, the question is: will it carry on moving in the same direction, or might it stop altogether and dissolve? Now it is true that we have large, fast and expensive computers able to calculate much regarding future development of the weather, but even their output still has, and will continue to have, an element of uncertainty – assessable only in retrospect. Even computers can produce only probable developments. This will perhaps make it comprehensible to the layman that, on the basis of a given weather situation the weatherman in one centre will assume that the front will dissolve on the way east, and forecast light southeasterlies with very isolated light showers. Another, say in Hamburg, considers that the front is going to become more active again and after a short pause will resume rapid and active movement. His forecast could then quite logically be: increasingly strong wind from the northwest with heavy gusty showers and thunderstorms. Total contradiction.

Usually one of the two will be correct, though it could happen that both are wide of the mark: then it's just a case of the atmosphere again dipping into its bag of tricks. Both meteorologists acted on the best of their knowledge at the time. Neither would have been able to prove to the other that of the two of them he was the one to assess the situation correctly: only time can provide that conclusion.

One final comment: when confronted by contradictory forecasts, *do not* just press on regardless, always suspect the worst.

Drawing and using weather maps based on the shipping forecasts

Most weather bulletins present a problem for the listener in that they contain too much information in too short a transmission time. A tape recorder, which can repeat the report until everyone on board has understood all of it, provides a good way out of this dilemma. Such repeated listening to the weather report makes a real contribution to safety. I'm sure

Weather map produced by the maritime weather office in Hamburg for on-board use.

everyone is familiar with the air of uncertainty on board when shortly after the broadcast someone says: 'Tell me, was the wind around Ushant still from the southwest or had it veered to northwest already?'

'Rubbish, Skagen surely has northwest force 5 – or was that Fornaes?' The tape gets you over that sort of problem. But there is one thing it cannot transmit: an understanding of the spatial distribution of the pressure formations. To envisage simultaneously everything alluded to in the weather situation, and whose significance has still to be assessed, is simply expecting too much from a lot of skippers. In addition, there is the problem of visualising up to 24 weather observations made by the stations.

If representation in the mind doesn't work, one has to simplify things a bit and help out by drawing an on-board weather map. This is made easier by using one of the prepared forms designed for recreational navigation and intended to illustrate shipping bulletins. There is space for writing down the bulletin, which is then marked on the associated map; with a bit of practice, anyone can do it. Please take a look at the original Deutschlandfunk report and forecast, which we are now going to evaluate just as if we were in harbour somewhere and had to decide whether to venture out and if so where to go.

---

16 April shipping bulletin at 0105 European Summer Time

Weather situation at 1900 yesterday:
High 1025 eastern Baltic weakening somewhat, wandering southeast.
Low 990 Jan Mayen moving northeast.
Secondary depression 1020 northern North Sea slewing eastwards.
Shallow low 1015 southern Germany little change.
High 1032 west of Biscay extending northwards.

Forecast until 1200 today

German Bight:	NE 3–4, hazy
Southwest North Sea:	winds light, hazy
Dogger:	NW 3–4, hazy
Fisher:	winds light, hazy
Skagerrak:	S 3, hazy
Kattegat:	SE 3, hazy
Western Baltic:	E 3–4, hazy
Central Baltic:	E 3–4, visibility moderate

Outlook until 2400 today

German Bight:	N to NW 4
Southwest North Sea:	N to NW 4
Dogger:	NW to W 4–5
Fisher:	N to NW 4
Skagerrak:	NW to W 4–5
Kattegat:	NW 4
Western Baltic:	winds light, later N 3–4
Central Baltic	winds light, later NW 4–5

As soon as you have written down
the whole of the report, start entering
it on the map.

Weather station reports at 2000 yesterday

		Wind	Weather	Temp. °C	Pressure
1.	Sklinna	S 6	hazy	6	1014
2.	Svinoy	SSW 5	showers	6	1016
3.	Lista	SE1	hazy	10	1021
4.	Aberdeen	SSE 1	hazy	9	1022
5.	Tynemouth	E 1	hazy	9	1022
6.	Hemsby	N 3	hazy	12	1022
7.	Den Helder	N 2	hazy	14	1020
8.	Borkum Riff	NE 4	hazy	8	1021
9.	Helgoland	NNE 2	hazy	10	1021
10.	List/Sylt	NNE 2		15	1021
11.	Thyboron	N 1		11	1021
12.	Skagen	SSE 1	hazy	9	1022
13.	Fornaes	SE 2	hazy	9	1022
14.	Kullen	SE 2		13	1023
15.	Kegnaes	ESE 4	hazy	8	1021
16.	Kiel-Holtenau	ESE 5		11	1021
17.	Puttgarden	E 4		9	1022
18.	LV Mön	SE 3		6	1024
19.	Arkona	E 3		7	1024
20.	Bornholm	SE 3		5	1025
21.	Visby	S 3		8	1023
22.	Mariehamn	SSW 3		3	1023
23.	Hel	NNE 2	hazy	4	1024
24.	WS L	W 4		8	1029
25.	Cherbourg	SW 2	hazy	14	1027

How a station's weather report is entered on the map

1. *Overwrite the station circle (here Svinoy, no. 2 in the list)*
2. *Draw the arrow for the wind direction: here SW*
3. *Add the Beaufort scale symbol: here force 5 (for every 2 force steps, 1 long stroke; for 1, a short stroke)*
4. *Air temperature is entered to the left of the station circle: here 10°C*
5. *Atmospheric pressure is to the right: here 1015 mbar (or hPa), omitting thousands and hundreds for simplicity.*
6. *Finally, enter the weather and visibility observed at the station at the lower right: here, showers.*

DLF-Sendung vom ....16.04........ 12.40, [01.05,] 06.40 Uhr GZ			
Wetterlage von Uhr	Stationsmeldungen vom Uhr	Vorhersagen bis heute 24 Uhr – heute 12 Uhr – heute 18 Uhr	Aussichten bis morgen 12 Uhr – heute 24 Uhr – morgen 06 Uhr
- gestern 19 Uhr			
Hoch 1025 östlich Ost= see etwas abschwächend, Südost wandernd, Tief 990 Jan Mayen nordost ziehend, Ausläufer 1020 nördliche Nordsee See ost-schwankend, flaches Tief 1015 Süd-deutschland wenig ändernd, Hoch 1032 westlich der Biskaya nordaus weitend.	1 Sklinna S6 diesig 1014	Deutsche Bucht	
	2 Svinöy SSW5 Schauer 6 1016	nordost 3-4 diesig	nord bis nordwest 4
	3 Lista SE1 diesig 10 1021		
	4 Aberdeen SSE1 diesig 9 1022	Südwestliche Nordsee (Humber, Themse)	
	5 Tynemouth E1 diesig 9 1022	schwachwindig, diesig	nord bis nordwest 4
	6 Hemsby N3 diesig 12 1022		
	7 Den Helder N2 diesig 14 1020	Fischer	
	8 FS Borkumriff NE4 diesig 8 1021	nordwest 3-4 diesig	nordwest bis west 4-5
	9 Helgoland NNE2 diesig 10 1021		
	10 List auf Sylt NNE2 15 1021		
	11 Thyboron N1 11 1021	Skagerrak	
	12 Skagen SSE1 diesig 9 1022	Süd 3 diesig	nordwest bis west 4-5
	13 Fornaes SE2 diesig 9 1022		
	14 Kullen SE2 13 1023	Kattegat	
	15 Kegnaes ESE4 diesig 8 1021	Südost 3 diesig	nordwest 4
	16 Kiel-Holtenau ESE5 11 1021		
	17 Puttgarden E4 9 1022	Belte und Sund	
	18 FS Mön SE3 6 1024	Ost 3-4 diesig	schwachwindig, später nord 3-4
	19 Arkona E3 7 1024		
	20 Bornholm SE3 5 1025		
	21 Visby S3 8 1023	Westliche Ostsee	
	22 Mariehamn SSW3 3 1023	Ost 3-4 diesig	schwachwindig, später nord 3-4
	23 Hel NNE2 diesig 4 1024		
	24 Ozeanwetterschiff L W4 8 1029	Südliche Ostsee	schwachwindig,
	25 Cherbourg SW6 bedeckt 15 1030	Ost 3-4 mittlere Sicht	später nordwest 4-5
SYMBOLE: = Sprühregen, • Regen, * Schnee, △ Graupel ▲ Hagel, ≡ diesig, ≡ Nebel, K Gewitter, ▽ Regenschauer, ▽ Schneeschauer, ⚡ Wetterleuchten + Schneetreiben			

The reverse of the map after writing in the shipping reports and forecast. Don't forget to insert the correct date and time at the top.

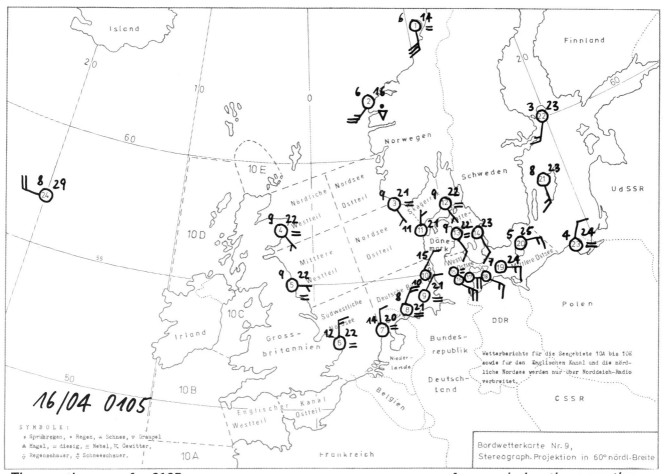

16/04 0105

SYMBOLE :
, Sprühregen, • Regen, * Schnee, ∇ Graupel
▲ Hagel, ∞ diesig, ≡ Nebel, ℞ Gewitter,
∇̇ Regenschauer, ∇̇ Schneeschauer.

Wetterberichte für die Seegebiete 10A bis 10E
sowie für den Englischen Kanal und die nörd-
liche Nordsee werden nur über Norddeich-Radio
verbreitet.

Bordwetterkarte Nr. 9,
Stereograph. Projektion in 60° nördl. Breite

**The weather map for 0105
when all station reports have
been entered.**

**As a reminder, these are the
most important weather symbols: doubled or tripled drizzle
and rain symbols mean 'moderate' or 'heavy'.**

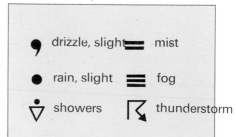

Unfortunately there is something confusing.

1. On weather maps you generally find the wind with its speed in knots indicated; the sole exception is the maps from the Hamburg maritime service which give Beaufort numbers.

2. The fleches on the wind-arrows thus provide differing information. To avoid banana-skins, you also use the Beaufort scale when drawing your on-board map.

Do that for all the reporting stations, and that's the first part of the job done. Make sure you use a non-erasable pen for the station entries: you'll see why when we get to the later part of the work.

How highs and lows are entered

Next, the centres of the high and low pressure formations are mapped: large **L** in the right place for every low; correspondingly an **H** for every high. Alongside the letters, enter the associated pressure; you need them at once for drawing the isobars. Sometimes the position of significant fronts is also given; that also is drawn on. To fix their position, maritime meteorologists like to use geographically notable points.

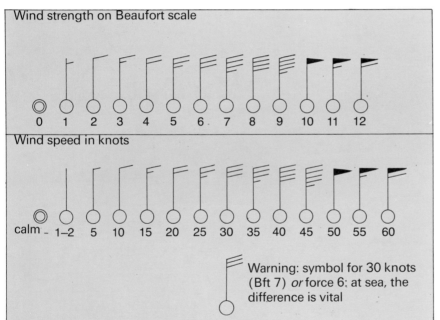

Wind strength on Beaufort scale
0 1 2 3 4 5 6 7 8 9 10 11 12

Wind speed in knots
calm 1-2 5 10 15 20 25 30 35 40 45 50 55 60

Warning: symbol for 30 knots (Bft 7) *or* force 6: at sea, the difference is vital

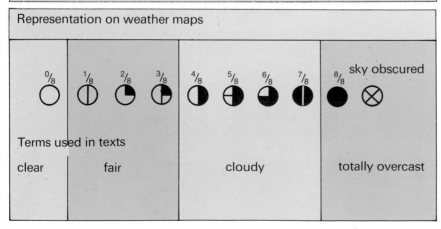

Representation on weather maps

0/8 1/8 2/8 3/8 4/8 5/8 6/8 7/8 8/8 sky obscured

Terms used in texts

clear | fair | cloudy | totally overcast

Amount of cloud cover of the sky

Cloud cover is stated in eighths, referred to the whole dome of the sky. In fog (or cloud down to sea level) the term 'sky obscured' is used.

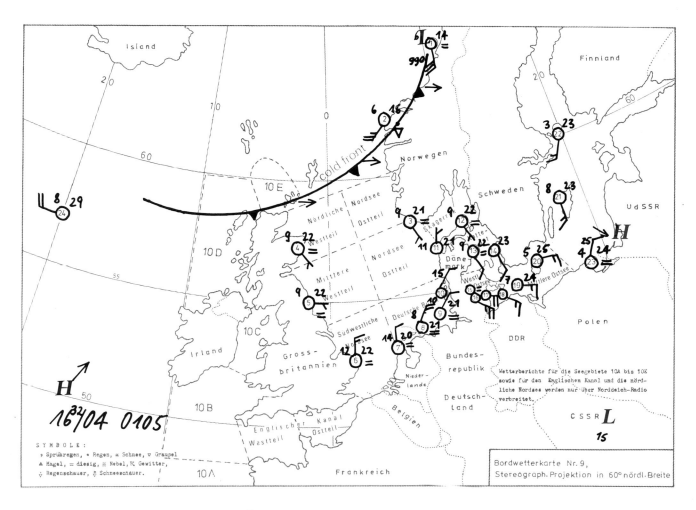

Bordwetterkarte Nr. 9,
Stereograph. Projektion in 60° nördl. Breite

When the positions of highs and lows have been added in the next stage of the work, the on-board map for 0105 looks like this

Drawing the isobars

Now we get to the part which most people find hard: how does one enter the isobars? In pencil, for the even-numbered mb draw one isobar, e.g. 1000, 1002, 1004 etc. Where English/American is spoken and also in some southern European countries, isobars are 2 or 4 mb apart, by convention. Elsewhere they may be 5 mb apart, as in this example.
● The closer together the isobars, the stronger the wind.

Around the high above the Baltic you can safely draw a line with 1025 mb. Bornholm there has the highest pressure with 1025 mb and is thus at the centre. Hela has 1 mb less so must not lie inside that circle. However since the centre of the high is said to be in the eastern Baltic, we extend the isobars in that direction. *Here, only the last two digits of the atmospheric pressure are entered against the isobars* to leave the picture clearer, that is 25 by the Bornholm isobar.

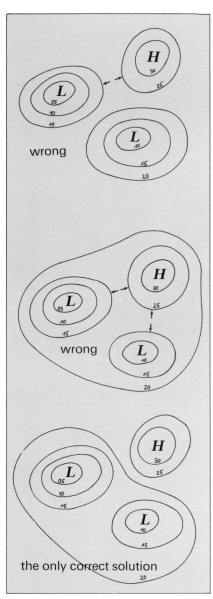

wrong

wrong

the only correct solution

Isobars drawn correctly and incorrectly

The Jan Mayen low we unfortunately cannot enter; the map does not extend that far. But since station 1 is closest to the low we can put in an isobar. Sklinna has 1014 mb so the 1015 line must lie south of there (farther from the low): it comes from the low and goes back to this again. The secondary depression mentioned is, as almost always, a cold front. It lies in the northern North Sea, but we don't just draw a line there, but rather extend it north towards the associated low. Now, which way?

Take a look at stations 1 and 2: it's right between these that the front runs through. That means Sklinna (1) is ahead of the front with a southerly wind and Svinoy (2) is already behind it, because the report says southwesterly winds with showers. Typical of the back of a cold front are the veered wind compared with that ahead of the front, and the shower activity which does not start until the front has passed.

Having identified the cold front, we draw it in up to the northern North sea. We know only approximately where the front is, because the sea area is large. One thing is sure, though: the front is north of station 3, because if it were south of it the wind there would have veered to SW-W. Also, it would then not be hazy at that station because cold and clear air flows in behind a cold front – no place for haziness. Somewhere west of Scotland you let the front end; here it matters little how far it is drawn in.

Now we enter the low over southern Germany: a bold **L** in a small circle with 15 added, for the pressure at the centre of the depression is said to be 1015 mb. The high west of Biscay lies outside the map, but so as not to lose this information entirely we write the **H** at its left-hand edge. If direction of movement is stated, we indicate this by an arrow: short arrows for slow movement, long ones for faster.

And now comes drawing in the remaining isobars – which causes the most difficulty. Between the high with 1032 mb and the weather ship L (24) with 1029, there must be a 1030 isobar which still belongs to the high. So we draw the 30 just south of station 24 and down into the Bay of Biscay.

Now for the south German low: since it is a shallow depression (synonymous with a small low) we already have a small 1015 isobar. The pressure around this low is bound to be higher so we can add another line for 1020. The only help we get is from the coastal station atmospheric pressures. Station 7 has precisely 1020 mb, so we make a single circuit around the shallow depression, passing directly through station 7. Distance from the other stations is increased depending on how much higher the pressure there is. This is called interpolation. An important indication of the direction and position of isobars is the wind reading at the stations. The direction of the wind arrows corresponds roughly with the run of the isobars; admittedly this rule applies only for winds above force 3 since light winds very often don't obey the atmospheric pressure distribution but rather obey local influences, such as the land-sea circulation.

For a complete picture of the isobars in the example, we lack another two. Between the low in the north and the high in the Baltic, a 1020 isobar is still missing. Of course it runs north of station 22, since 1023 mb was measured there, so we draw a bold curve from the top edge towards station 3 but staying north

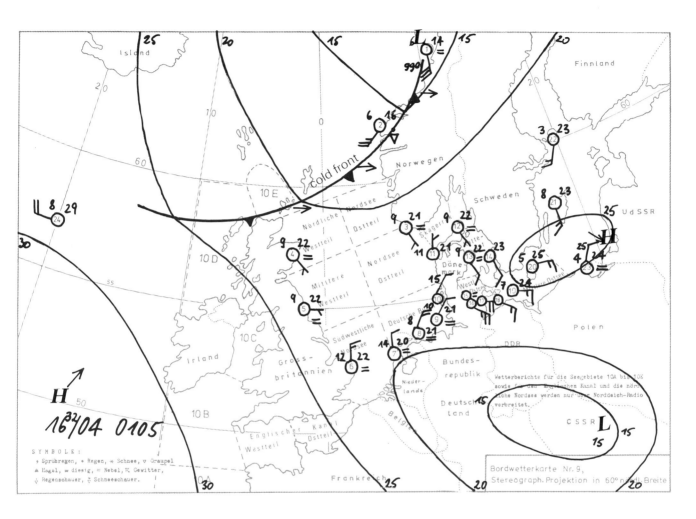

How the isobars run, according to the station reports

of this and on to the front from which we turn north again with a slight kink – back towards the low. Now still missing is a 1025 between the south German low and the Atlantic high The precise position of this isobar cannot be determined, so draw it about equidistant from the others. That really completes the weather map – at least the first draft, for now we go on to do something for appearance. To begin with your isobars will be a bit bumpy: rub out unnecessary kinks and even out the

spacing a bit, then redraw the final version with a soft pencil to make a thick line. While rubbing out you will notice why the station reports were entered with a ballpoint or felt pen: erasing and redrawing the isobars would otherwise have wiped away everything of importance. Finally a bit of colour: all Hs are coloured blue and all Ls red; cold fronts are also blue and if you do get to draw a warm front that will be red. Where precipitation is reported, take a green crayon and hatch the surroundings

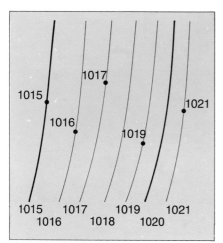

Interpolating isobars

The isobar spacing must reflect the pressure differences. If there are enough reports, isobars can be drawn for every mb.

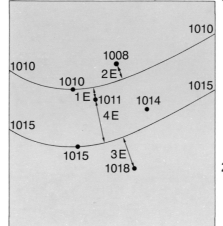

Draw the 1010 isobar so that it is 2 units away from the station with 1008 mb and precisely 1 unit from 1011 mb.
E = unit

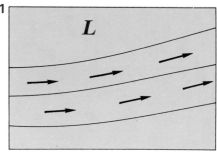

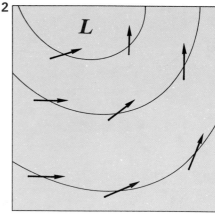

Isobars and direction of wind

1. Straight isobars: the air moves parallel to the isobars.

2. Curved isobars: the more pronounced the curvature, the larger the angle at which the air flows towards them.
All deflections are greater over land than over the sea.

of the station a bit. Haze and fog are yellow. Now the weather map is finished.

If you have to do a lot of rubbing out to begin with, don't despair – that's quite usual. After a few days practice you'll be doing this quite quickly. Should you get a map with a large range of pressures, giving rise to more isobars, you will find it easier to draw in every second one to begin with. Finally, when the map is finished it's got to have date and time on it, large and clear: they are very important. With several maps, it can easily happen during a cruise that someone starts working with the wrong one.

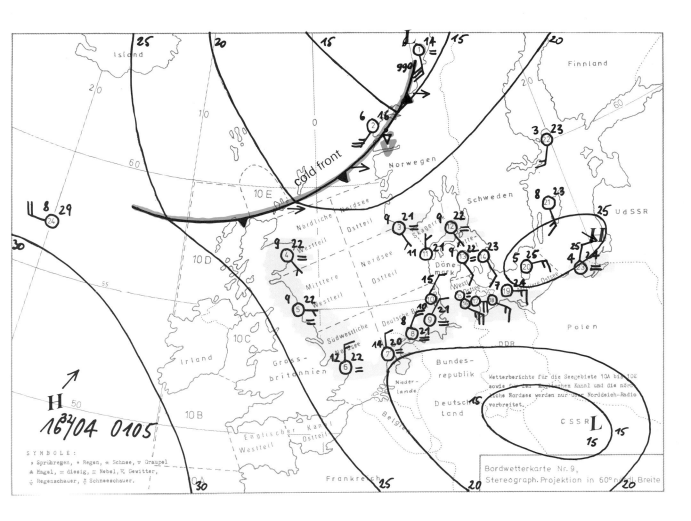

*How the weather map based
on the 1604 shipping bulletin
should look like when completed.*

Already out of date, but . . .

You have laboured nobly at doing
this map, but please don't get into a
rage if I tell you that it is already
about 4 hours old, for the weather
situation recorded (called surface
weather analysis) is that for 3 o'clock
in the morning. This cannot be
pointed out too often, because if you
don't take that factor into account
you can have a lot of problems. We
shall discuss this in more detail
shortly when you get to learn how to

formulate a forecast from the weather situation.

We have to live with the fact that *every* weather map is already of historical interest almost as soon as it's printed or drawn. It is nonetheless of considerable practical value because it represents a weather balance at a known time. Only if one has understood the initial situation can one also understand the forecast which develops out of it. Most developments in the atmosphere fortunately are not so rapid that everything has changed totally after 4 hours; however it is precisely the situations embodying danger which can develop with fantastic speed. They are also often behind wrong forecasts, because weather developments at such speeds can 'get away' even from the met men.

When your on-board weather map is finished, there is one advantage which you have over the weather man, and which you use. He has during the night produced a forecast based on a state of knowledge which now is already some hours old – and possibly has been overtaken by developments. The weather has carried on developing, so that you in the morning have access to more information than the professional had earlier in the night. Make a habit of observing continuously: an understanding of (and also feeling for) the weather makes an important contribution to the safety of boat and crew. Of course you can't acquire a feeling for weather until you understand how it tends to develop: don't place too much trust in inspiration. So supplement the entries on your newly-drawn map with your own observations in the form of a station report. *Thus your position also is clearly marked on the map.* This is important, because it allows you to

see much better which developments are heading for you. For planning a day's run, the forecast until 1800 with the outlook until 0600 in the morning is very suitable. However bear in mind that if the forecast for the day is already up the creek, the outlook will miss the mark by even more.

● A frequent mistake: if you move your highs and lows in accordance with the reports, in time they will vanish off the edge of the map. Some skippers use this to convert a 24-hour forecast into one of their own for two or three days ahead. That is wrong: all it is suitable for is sweeping the map clean pretty quickly. New developments moving in from the Atlantic make nonsense of such a method.

● A trick for entering pressure formations, which also helps with their movement. As 1° of latitude corresponds exactly to 60 n. miles (M), if the shipping bulletin talks about a low 400 M south of Iceland, you can quite easily enter that on the on-board weather map because 400 M corresponds exactly to 6.7° of latitude (400 ÷ 60). The low is thus 6.7° south of Iceland on the map.

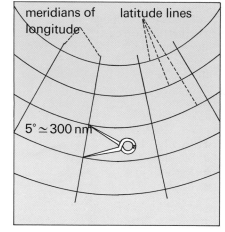

Measurement of nautical miles on the weather map.

Using any line of longitude, the latitude difference is measured with a compass.

1° difference in latitude ≃ 60 nm. Formula: Distance in degrees of latitude = distance in nm/60

The speed of movement of highs and lows

In general, high-pressure regions move slowly. They are rarely fast moving, and if on occasion the pressure does rise rapidly it means a change for the better in the weather. But how fast do lows move? Well, any speed from zero to 60 knots is on the cards. To obtain the actual rate of movement you have to rely entirely on the information from the shipping bulletin; it is not possible to make one's own forecast with on-board means. However, what you can do is to check continuously whether the forecast movement is in fact occurring, by comparing the weather development with that of the atmospheric pressure: both must chime with the forecast.

In UK practice, the terminology used has specific meanings:

- Slowly – less than 15 knots
- Steadily – 15–25 knots
- Rather quickly – 25–35 knots
- Rapidly – 35–45 knots
- Very rapidly – more than 45 knots

Rapidly developing storm depressions frequently move at a rate of 40–60 knots.

When evaluating the on-board weather map and the shipping bulletin, you must always bear in mind that this information presents only a crude picture of the actual conditions. The transmission-time constraint alone restricts mention of pressure formations to the most important ones. Sometimes it is not at all easy for the meteorologist to decide which is the most important – yet another reason for making your own careful observations. The sea area covered by recreational craft in the course of a single day is naturally very restricted, so they must attach great importance to the relevant local phenomena which the general report cannot take into account. Inshore weather forecasts and special services for major port areas obtainable by telephone from local centres are useful. Almanacs list these: note that some simply report conditions without forecasting.

Make use of the pre-season to practise at home. Draw your home weather maps and watch the weather development through the day. The daily conclusion to this exercise should be the late evening televised weather map and discussion. Continue the process over several days.

> *Exercise:*
> *Where does the cold front mentioned in the 16.04 weather report (above) lie 3, 6, 9, 12 hours later, if it is moving eastwards at 15–20 knots?*

Displacement of a low

A low said, for example, to be moving at 25 knots can be displaced using a compass, and thus shown to be lying off Göteborg in the Kattegat in 24 hours' time.

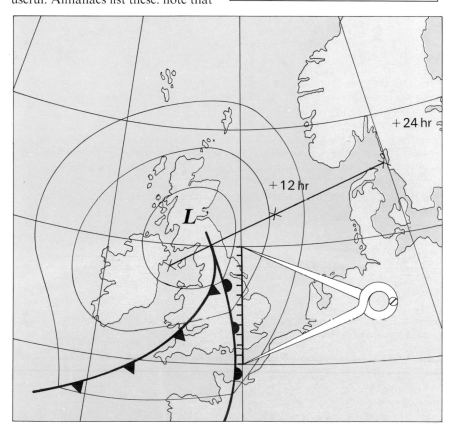

Interpreting your own weather map

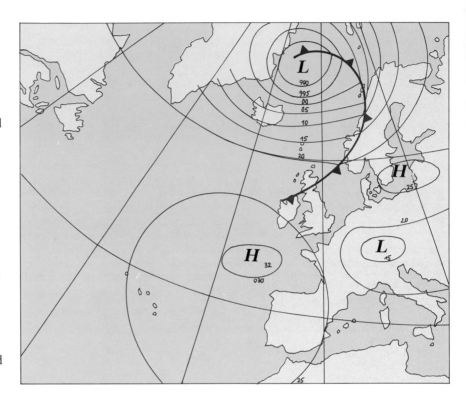

When drawing the first maps you will have noticed that unfortunately only a very small part of the overall weather situation can be shown on the map. On an appropriately large-scale map, it is of course easy to represent the Atlantic weather situation adequately. The sort of map shown here serves this purpose: the various pressure systems are easily visible, and what's going on in the Atlantic, but this scale falls down when you want to enter the many stations around the British Isles, North Sea and Baltic, and analyse the situation there.

In order not to neglect the large-scale weather structure, I recommend drawing an additional synoptic map showing as many of the pressure formations as possible. That doesn't take long, and appropriate printed forms are available. With a water-proof plastic cover you can re-draw the situation daily using a felt pen. At this point you may think: well now, I have learnt how to draw a weather map, but what does one do with it?

Using the weather situation of 14 November, I should like now to show you step-by-step how a weather map is evaluated.

The first part is always an introduction to the weather situation, of which one must have a good mental picture. Just the distribution of highs and lows doesn't tell you much. Slap in the middle of a low there may be sunshine and a flat calm, and in the adjoining high there is a gale blowing or it's raining cats and dogs – that's

how little the weather depends on the atmospheric pressure. This cannot be emphasized often enough: there is no

14 November shipping bulletin

Weather situation at 0400 today
    Storm 958 Arctic Ocean,
    moving NE slowly.
    Further storm 975, 400 nm
    south of Iceland, deepening,
    moving ENE.
    Low 980 west of Iceland,
    stationary.
    High 1037, Hungary, little
    change.
    High 1036, western France,
    moving eastwards.

This is what the weather situation at 1900 on 15.04 (see page 87) looks like when transferred to a synoptic-scale (without stations). The reports usually include more, and more remote, pressure centres than can be accommodated on the usual printed map forms.

physical connection between the value of the atmospheric pressure and the weather; only the measure of the pressure change influences its development. If you want to form a picture of the weather-activity of a pressure system, you have to have the station reports.

Forecast until 1800 today
German Bight: SW 7, increasing 8, visibility good.
Southwest North Sea: SW increasing 7–8, visibility moderate.
Fisher: SW increasing 8, visibility initially
                        good, showers.
Skagerrak: SW 6, later increasing 7–8, showery
                        gusts, visibility otherwise good.
Kattegat: SW increasing 6–7, visibility moderate.
Western Baltic: SW 6–7, later increasing somewhat,
                        visibility moderate to good.

Outlook until 0600 tomorrow
German Bight: SW 8, veering.
Southwest North Sea: SW to W 7–8, veering.
Fisher: SW–W 8, showery gusts.
Skagerrak: SW 8, showery gusts.
Kattegat: SW–W around 6, showery gusts.
Western Baltic: SW 7.

Weather reports time 0400 this morning

	Wind	Weather	Temp. °C	Pressure
1. Sklinna	W 6	rain	8	997
2. Svinoy	W 6	showers	8	1009
3. Lista	WSW 6		9	1014
4. Aberdeen	S 4	rain	7	1008
5. Tynemouth	S 4	cloudy	9	1015
6. Hemsby	SW 4	7/8 cloud	9	1027
7. Den Helder	SW 5		10	1027
8. Borkum Riff	SW 5		10	1025
9. Helgoland	SW 6		10	1025
10. Lyst/Sylt	SWS 5		11	1023
11. Thyboron	W 6		11	1016
12. Skagen	WSW 5	showers	8	1015
13. Fornaes	SW 4		7	1018
14. Kullen	W 6	showers	8	1019
15. Kegnaes	SW 5		9	1023
16. Kiel-Holtenau	SW 5	no obser-vation	8	1026
17. Puttgarden	—	—	—	—
18. LV Mön	SW 4	misty	6	1026
19. Arkona	WSW 5	misty	5	1026
20. Bornholm	W 7		9	1023
21. Visby	SW5	misty	9	1019
22. Marihamn	SSW 3	misty	7	1015
23. Hel	SW 4	misty	8	1025
24. WS L	WSW 8	showers	14	987
25. Cherbourg	SW 6	cloudy	15	1030

Weather situation on 14. 11.

For a quick overview it helps if the weather situation is sketched in broadly and only a few station reports are entered. To simplify things, only isobars at 10 mb spacing are drawn, and station temperature reports are omitted.

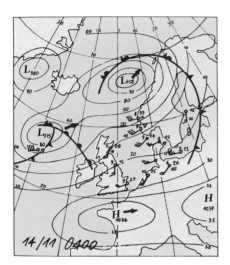

The complete (large-sale synoptic) on-board weather map for 14.11.

If the run of secondary depressions is not stated precisely, it can only be sketched in roughly. On a synoptic map of such a large scale, only a limited amount of weather information can be accommodated.

How the complete weather picture for 14.11 looks on the smaller scale map.

This map offers more, but less wide-ranging, weather information – which is what we need on board. A comparison of the two maps clearly indicates the advantages and disadvantages of the two different scales. In westerly conditions, where lows and rain fronts pass through in rapid succession, the large-scale map is a valuable aid to orientation.

The map The storm over the Arctic Ocean should move slowly northeastwards. The air flowing in behind it is fresh sea air, since the isobars come from the Atlantic and the North Sea which means that the air also is coming from there. Station Skagen lies in the middle of this air mass, for it has showers with a west wind. The cold front not specifically mentioned in the report must already lie well to the east, since even Bornholm has a strong westerly breeze. The weather in our sea area will soon be determined by the storm currently south of Iceland. If this storm moves into the Norwegian Sea as forecast, there is going to be a struggle for dominance along the German coast between the still predominant high and the storm-associated cold fronts. For sailors near the coast, the question is, how far south are these fronts going to

extend – i.e. to what extent is this new low going to change the weather?

In the Baltic there is a lot of haze, which means the high atmospheric pressure of the European Continental high still dominates there. Along its northwestern side, muggy air from warmer regions is being brought in. Since in a high the general motion of the air mass is downwards, water vapour arising from spray, evaporation or man-made cannot be transported away; on the contrary, everything collects in the layer of air next the surface and causes visibility to deteriorate. This mist or haze can even deteriorate into fog which even quite a lot of wind cannot always blow away. If near the coast this high-pressure influence abates because the storm is approaching, you will be made aware of this quite clearly by the improving visibility.

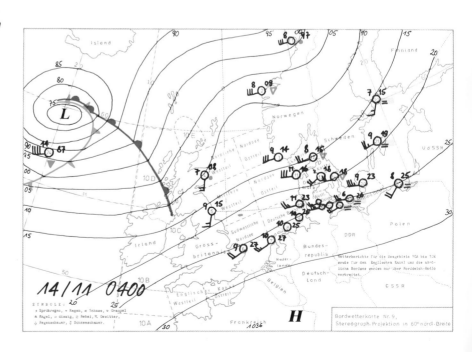

Between the departing low over the Arctic Ocean and the storm south of Iceland there must be a small intermediate-high ridge. If you observe the direction of the wind along the east coast of Britain, you will see that the isobars there have to run south a bit before they bend around towards the storm. That indicates an intermediate high ridge, which typically also lies ahead of warm fronts. The more marked the depression with its fronts, the more clearly will this intermediate high ahead of the warm front gradually form. In our example the ridge is going to strengthen further – which means a passing, but deceptive, improvement in the weather since once the ridge has passed you the warm front with rain and wind will arrive.

As yet the entire German coast is under the influence of that mighty high, but one can already see the signs of the deceptive intermediate-high weather (see 'Practical weather-rules'). Compared with the others, the British coast stations experience the typical backing of the wind ahead of a front (caused by the small ridge); at the same time the wind has dropped noticeably compared with Heligoland and Elbe 1. It is already raining in Aberdeen: the warm front can't be far away. You can safely sketch in a warm front a bit to the west of that station. The low to the west of Iceland is only the miserable remains of a once powerful storm: there is no need to map it.

Now we have really extracted everything from the weather situation that the report has contributed. The meteorologist calls this exercise 'analysing'. Though this example actually occurred in the late autumn, it is nevertheless typical for July and August when westerlies prevail in our regions. That also accounts for the unsettled summers, all too often rained off.

Own-weather observations

Our next step is to examine the meteorologist's forecast to see how he envisaged the further development. Although he has a lot more information about the weather situation and its development, we are able to add later what the actual change has been. Understanding that, we are then right on top of the weather. Should it develop other than as forecast, not only do we notice it in good time but also we have some idea of what has caused the change. That allows us to adjust quickly to the new conditions – long before the next shipping bulletin, which only notes the changed conditions much later. The principle is to use a certain amount of basic knowledge together with careful observation.

Let's assume you are lying in Heligoland, and have recorded this shipping bulletin at 0640 and drawn your on-board weather map. So towards 8 a.m. you carry out a weather observation of your own:

Sky: overcast
Visibility: good
Barometer: dropped steadily to 1022 mb
Wind: southerly, force 5

This shows that you are already right in the intermediate-high ridge – indeed, already in the second half with a worsening trend. You can tell that from the steadily falling pressure and the backing to south of the wind which has also dropped somewhat since the night. If the barometer is dropping by 1 mb or more per hour, a careful eye needs to be kept on it. Either the low will come slowly towards you, or it will pass by to the north – but then it need not move slowly. In this case the latter applies, since it was referred to as a storm and they rarely move slowly when they are still young and thus small in extent.

So we can record: compared with the situation at 0400 the pressure has dropped noticeably, the sky has becomed cloudy and is now totally overcast. The wind has barely changed. So far, that all fits in with the forecast; you can assume that both forecast and outlook will turn out to be correct. The wind is due to increase to force 8 and veer, which means that the warm front is going to cross the North Sea. But since no precipitation has been forecast for the German Bight, the warm front is going to stay north of it, say north of 55°, which is the boundary between the German Bight and the central North Sea.

At this point you should notice a minor contradiction between the forecast and the weather you observed at Heligoland: if the warm front is not due to extend into the German Bight, it is curious that already in the morning there is such thick cloud cover, which is an indication of an approaching front. So assume that the front will reach down to the German North Sea coast – which of course implies a worsening of the weather compared with the forecast, because there will be rain with poor visibility and possibly even more wind.

In the same way as I have demonstrated how to interpret the weather situation and the forecast, you also will be able to do this with a bit of practice. Just be careful in your interpretation of the shipping bulletin and with your own observations. To give you some practice, let us now look at the next day: then you will also see how the weather really did develop.

Draw the on-board weather map in accordance with the shipping bulle-

Weather situation on 15.11.

The map you drew on the basis of the situation report for 15.11 ought to look like this.

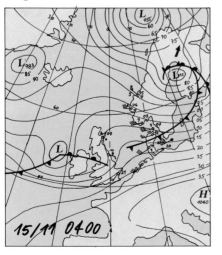

15/11 0400

tin. You've already had some practice so I can be briefer. From the outlook until 16 November you can deduce that the storm-associated cold front will not cross the North Sea until the night (based on talk of veering to NW while dropping slightly). The Baltic should then come under the influence of the cold front in the second half of the night.

So much for the development as it should be after the 15th. Now we check whether what was forecast on the 14th for the 15th really hap-

pened. Look at the station reports:
1. At 0400 on the 15th it was raining at three stations, entirely contrary to the forecast. One can assume that it was raining around these stations as well. The contradiction is easily explained on the basis of what was already indicated the day before: the warm front did extend somewhat farther south than had been assumed.
2. The wind forecast for the North Sea did not come true: instead of veering to the northwest it

Weather reports for 0400 on 15 November	Wind	Weather	Temp. °C	Pressure
1. Sklinna	WNW 5	showers	5	999
2. Svinoy	W 6	showers	6	1006
3. Lista	W 7	showers	7	1009
4. Aberdeen	S 2	rain	6	1009
5. Tynemouth	ESE 3	rain	7	1010
6. Hemsby	SSW 4	–	11	1021
7. Den Helder	SSW 6	–	12	1022
8. Borkum Riff	SW 7	–	12	1021
9. Helgoland	SW 6	foggy	12	1020
10. List/Sylt	SWS 6	drizzle	11	1017
11. Thyboron	SW 7	misty	9	1008
12. Skagen	W 8	–	9	1007
13. Fornaes	W 5	–	10	1012
14. Kullen	WSW 8	rain	11	1015
15. Kegnaes	WSW 7	misty	11	1017
16. Kiel-Holtenau	WSW 7	–	10	1020
17. Puttgarden	WSW 6	–	10	1020
18. LV Mön	WSW 7	–	10	1020
19. Arkona	WSW 8	–	10	1018
20. Bornholm	WSW 8	–	10	1015
21. Visby	W 6	rain	8	1004
22. Mariehamn	W 9	showers	5	992
23. Hel	WSW 7	misty	7	1015
24. WS L	SW 5	–	12	1003
25. Cherbourg	SW 6	–	13	1026

intermediate-high ridge ahead of the warm front. So it all starts again from the beginning – typical wester-lies situation.

Summarizing:

How to work with your on-board weather map

1. Write down the complete shipping bulletin including all station reports.
2. Enter the station reports on the map (eraser-proof).
3. Mark the pressure centres.
4. Draw in the isobars (say 4 mb apart initially, for greater clarity).
5. Apply colours.
6. Evaluate = interpret: add movement arrows and compare the map with the shipping forecast.
   – How must the situation as drawn change, to make the meteorologist's forecast come true?
   – What kind of weather is to be expected during the day?

remained from SW. Why? The peripheral low near Ireland rapidly developed out of the storm-associated cold front and thereby created a lot of chaos.
3. In the Baltic things happened as forecast. The three stations with the lighter wind are shielded by the land mass and in the lee of the coast. From the run, and also the spacing, of the isobars over Skagerrak, Kattegat and Baltic it is quite clear that the wind strength at sea must be the same everywhere.

For the further development of the weather, we must now take a look at the new peripheral low near Ireland, which was responsible for the erroneous forecast. That this young low will develop further you can already deduce from the buildup of a hefty

Weather facsimile maps

All those concerned agree that the current supply of weather information leaves a great deal to be desired – yet a revolutionary device for yachtsmen has quietly become established on the market: the on-board weather map printer or weather fax. Today's printers can take up no more space than a portable radio. Current consumption is of the order of 1–2 amps; typically a fax used only 380 mA when operating.

There is a considerable range in prices and specification. Depending on the type, they are either connected to the existing radio receiver or have their own integral receiver. Having a weather map printer solves all the earlier problems of information supply. There are no more language difficulties: symbols used are international. If you happen to miss a transmission, simply switch to another transmitter from which you will get the same or a similar map a bit later.

In every European sea area one can receive at least three different weather map transmitting stations.

The advantages of weather fax
● The visual presentation has an important effect on understanding and utility.
● No language problem.
● Information cannot get lost.

- Wide choice of transmission times around the clock.
- Great success as teaching medium by virtue of interpretation and comparison of maps.
- The possibility of going over the weather in retrospect.

How a fax printer works

All major nations which have weather services also broadcast. The weather maps are broadcast daily in accordance with a fixed transmission plan, so that all you do is set your receiver to the station frequency. Everything else technically necessary for reception is dealt with by the electronics in the printer.

Before a station begins to broadcast the map, it transmits a starting signal which activates the printer. So that the platen operates with the same 'rhythm' as that of the transmitter, the on-board receiver also gets a synchronizing signal. Then the automatic drawing of the map begins; it is stopped by the transmitter as soon as the map is completed.

Using weather fax maps

The principal times for weather observation world-wide and thus for weather maps are 0000, 0600, 1200 and 1800 Universal Coordinated Time (UTC-like GMT, radio abbreviation Z).

The weather map produced in a met office is based on hundreds of simultaneous observations, expertly analysed. Such an analysis is the foundation for an understanding of the current weather, and of course the forecast.

The isobars and fronts are a significant part of the analysis map.

Naturally pressure centres and fronts seldom remain where analysis has located them at a given point in time. Having a weather map printer, you are able to take on board the weather centre's projection of the isobar and front location. The weather services daily broadcast surface forecast maps for $T + 24$, $T + 48$, $T + 72$, i.e. one to three days ahead. Should one of these forecasts go awry, an individual, however experienced, could not have done any better.

The simplest way of catching up with the weather is thus:

1. Recording a **surface weather analysis** of the weather as it actually occurred.
2. Recording a **surface weather forecast** of the probable further development.

Even with only these two maps, one is miles ahead of any shipping bulletin if one can interpret them correctly. One sees in detail how fronts move, how pressure formations shift and change the weather: all one needs to do is look at the two maps side-by-side.

The weather fax printer fits into pratically any navigation space. Here you can work on charts and weather maps in peace and quiet: 'meteorological navigation' then can be everyday practice.

The most important weather symbols

In all weather analysis maps either symbols or figures are used that have the same meaning world-wide. You need not know all of these, which are those used most.

⌐ visibility reduced by industrial fumes

∞ dry haze, from dust or smoke

═ mist; haze of water droplets

_ _ shallow fog (up to about 2 m deep)

⟨ sheet lightning

Ɽ thunderstorm without precipitation

∀ strong gust

)(wind/waterspout

⤳ sandstorm

Types of rain:

⦁ precipitation which does not reach the ground (re-evaporates)

)•(precipitation more than 5 km from the station

(•) precipitation less than 5 km from the station

, light
; medium   intermittent drizzle
; heavy

" light
," medium   continuous drizzle
," heavy

; light
; medium   rain and drizzle mixed
to heavy

• light
: medium   intermittent rain
: heavy

•• light
•:• medium   continuous rain
•:• heavy

▽ light shower

⧩ very heavy shower

⬦ sleet shower

⧨ hail shower

Thunderstorms

Ɽ thunderstorm with rain

Ɽ thunderstorm with hail or sleet

Ⱳ heavy thunderstorm with rain

Ⱳ heavy thunderstorm with hail or sleet

Fog

≡ fog

_≡_ damp fog

≡| fog which has thinned (within past hour)

≡ fog unchanged during past hour

|≡ fog which has thickened during past hour

A supplementary symbol

If a weather feature has been observed within the hour before the reporting-time but has since ceased, the symbol is boxed:

Atmospheric pressure tendency

The reference period is always the 3 hours before the reporting time. Since observations world-wide are made, and a surface weather map with station reports is broadcast, every 3 hours, this gives you a good picture of the atmospheric pressure changes.

∧ first rising, latterly falling

⌐/ first rising, then remaining constant

/ rising steadily

√ first falling, then rising

— remaining steady

∨ first falling, then rising

⌐\ first falling, then remaining constant

\ falling steadily

∧ rising initially, then falling

Code for visibility

Here you have to be careful: two different codes are being used simultaneously.

Ships' code for visibility

90 up to 50 m
91 >   50 m
92 >   200 m
93 >   500 m
94 >   1 km

95 >	2 km
96 >	4 km
97 >	10 km
98 >	20 km
99 >	50 km

Land use code for visibility
00 up to 0,1km
01 ≧ 01, km
02 ≧ 0,2 km

Rule: for 01–49, in the two-digit figure insert a comma between the digits: that is the visibility in km.
48 = 4,8 km
49 = 4,9 km
50 = 5,0 km

Rule: for 56–59, if you leave off the 5 the remaining digit gives the visibility in km.
56 = 6 km
57 = 7 km
58 = 8 km
59 = 9 km

Rule: for 61–69, leave off the first 6: the remaining digit + 10 gives the visibility in km.
60 = 10 km
61 = 11 km
62 = 12 km

69 = 19 km

Rule: for 70–80, as for figures in 50s and 60s.
70 = 20 km
71 = 21 km

78 = 28 km
80 = 30 km

The code above 80 is unimportant for boating. Just remember that figures above 80 indicate visibility exceeding 30 km.

Note
Some shore stations also use the simpler ships' code.

Symbols for types of cloud
Corresponding precisely to the three levels of cloud, you will find the cloud symbols at these levels in the station data. Low cloud is underneath the station circle, middle cloud above. Exactly above the latter are the symbols for high level clouds.

Low clouds:

small cumulus **(fair weather cumulus)**

medium size cumulus

large cumulus **(shower type)**

stratocumulus

cumulus and stratocumulus, mixed

cumulonimbus (Cb) **(rain and thunder)**

stratus and rags of cumulus **(foul weather type)**

pure stratus

cumulus and stratocumulus at different heights

Middle level clouds:

altostratus; the sun still shines through

thick altostratus and/or nimbostratus; sun no longer to be seen, **foul weather type**

altocumulus

special forms of altocumulus

altocumulus with altostratus and/or nimbostratus, **foul weather type**

altocumulus, **thunder cloud**

altocumulus 'chaotic sky', **threatening foul weather**

High clouds

cirrus

cirrus building up, **foul weather type**

cirrostratus building up, **foul weather type**

cirrostratus, sun shines through, halo

cirrocumulus, fair weather type

These clouds bring bad weather:

?222ₛ_ₛ   at high level

M ϛ ω ⫽ ∠ ∽   at middle level

⌷ — - - -   at low level

107

The analysis you can recognize at once, even should the legend along the map edge have got lost in transmission: there is a multitude of station reports all over the map, which is full of highs, lows and fronts. They show in detail what sort of weather conditions the stations have reported for their vicinity. A most important piece of advice: whatever else, establish the date/time of the map clearly. Maps without this are totally useless.

Weather code symbols

The complete observation at a weather station is coded into numbers and symbols and then printed onto the analysis map. This is done by computer, in the weather service centre. Only a little practice is sufficient for finding one's way through the apparent maze of data: to begin with, concentrate on only a few elements of the station report.

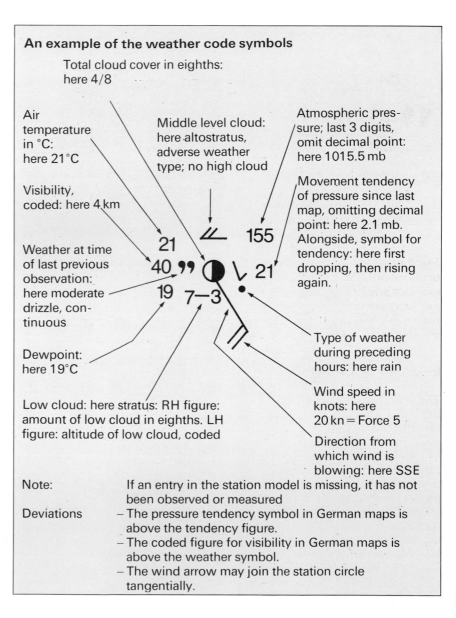

An example of the weather code symbols

Total cloud cover in eighths: here 4/8

Air temperature in °C: here 21°C

Middle level cloud: here altostratus, adverse weather type; no high cloud

Atmospheric pressure; last 3 digits, omit decimal point: here 1015.5 mb

Visibility, coded: here 4 km

Movement tendency of pressure since last map, omitting decimal point: here 2.1 mb. Alongside, symbol for tendency: here first dropping, then rising again.

Weather at time of last previous observation: here moderate drizzle, continuous

Dewpoint: here 19°C

Low cloud: here stratus: RH figure: amount of low cloud in eighths. LH figure: altitude of low cloud, coded

Type of weather during preceding hours: here rain

Wind speed in knots: here 20 kn = Force 5

Direction from which wind is blowing: here SSE

Note: If an entry in the station model is missing, it has not been observed or measured

Deviations — The pressure tendency symbol in German maps is above the tendency figure.
— The coded figure for visibility in German maps is above the weather symbol.
— The wind arrow may join the station circle tangentially.

An actual weather report from the map

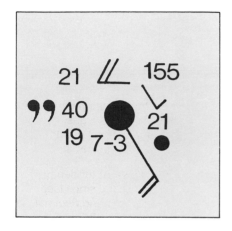

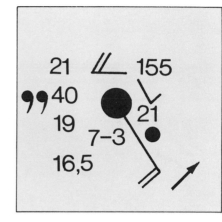

Such station reports look pretty complicated. The yacht skipper should concern himself exclusively with the information which is of importance to small craft.

Reading the symbolized report

The sky is totally covered (8/8); the low cloud is stratus with ragged cumulus (symbol – –) of the adverse-weather type. The two figures 7 and 3 by the cloud symbol are of no significance for yachtsmen. The middle cloud is nimbostratus, providing precipitation. No high cloud observed. The wind is blowing from the SE at 20 kt which the conversion table makes equal to force 5. Air temperature 21°C, dewpoint 19°C. Visibility 4 km coded as 40. Atmospheric pressure 1015.5 mb; in the past few hours it first dropped sharply (by

2.1 mb) but then rose again. In the last hours before the observation it has been raining; now it is still drizzling. From this mass of data, selecting those aspects important to a yachtsman reduces it to a few pieces of important information (above centre):
– Wind direction and strength
– Weather events
– Visibility
– Pressure and its tendency

Weather report from a ship

Station report from a ship
Station reports from ships are even more laborious than those from shore. They give the water temperature, shown bottom left relative to the station and recognizable by always having a decimal point (comma). At bottom right an arrow indicates which way the ship is sailing. Ships use the special 90s code (90 to 99) for visibility.

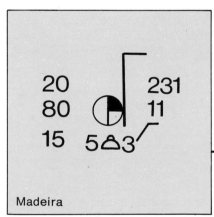

20
80
15 5△3

231
11

Madeira

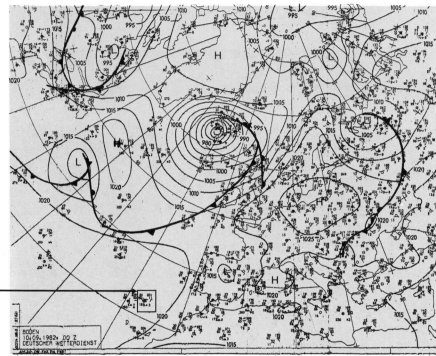

Surface weather analysis, Europe and North Atlantic

This is the scaled-down original of a weather map as produced by the on-board weather fax printer. It is a surface weather analysis at 0000 UCT (=Z) on 10 Sept 1982, from the German weather service. As well as the isobars and fronts, the map shows a multitude of station reports each comprising a complete, partially coded, weather observation based on the principles already

explained. To make the reports clear and easily found, the coast contours are merely sketched in. Familiarisation with weather maps takes less practice than it might appear.

Let's see what sort of weather Madeira has reported (in the box): 10 knot (Bft 3) northerly wind, cloud over about half the sky (3/8), air temperature 20°C, the dewpoint (which doesn't concern us) 15°C. Visibility (80) is 30 km. Atmospheric pressure stands at 1023.1 and since the

last reporting time has risen by 1.1 mb. But most recently it has remained constant. Cloud: cumulus (fair weather type) at 3/8 in altitude 5 (altitude is not important for us).

If the weather maps are drawn by computer, for technical reasons the wind-direction arrow is drawn tangentially to the station circle.

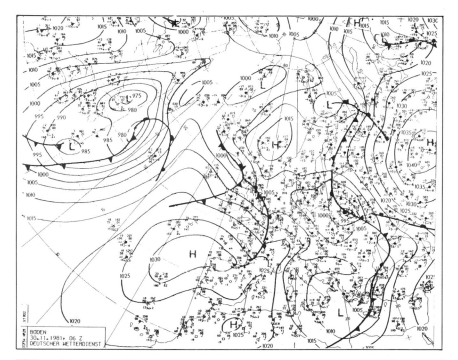

Surface weather analysis for 0600 on 30.11. as printed out on weather fax. It contains a complete analysis of the European and Atlantic weather situation, compiled from millions of items of weather data from over a huge area.

The basis for understanding the weather, either present or future, is a careful analysis of the available data and findings, as put out every 6 hours or so by the weather services. Let us then start work with the weather fax. First, we interpret the situation as presented to us in analysis form timed 0600Z (Z = UTC) on 30 November.

Reading the weather map

Two extensive lows with lengthy fronts mainly dominate the weather. The low over Poland with a core pressure of 995 mb influences the Baltic sea areas and a little pocket of isobars (trough) even extends into the Kattegat. I'm sure you remember that such bulges in the isobars associated with a low bring bad weather.

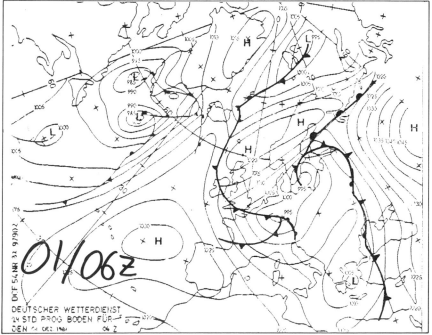

Surface forecast for 0600 on 1.12. This is what a weather forecast map received by on-board fax looks like. It was broadcast directly from the German weather service's computer centre. The forecast map shows in full detail how highs and lows are due to move from their earlier reported positions.

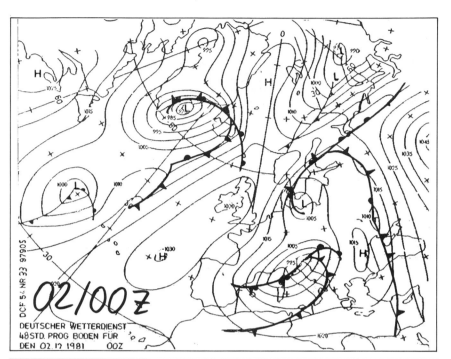

Surface forecast for 0000 on 2.12.

A further low with 970 mb lies between Scotland and Iceland. Its gaping warm sector covers the whole of the British Isles. Typically, ahead of the warm front we find an intermediate-high ridge which thus temporarily brings better weather to parts of France and western Germany. The Mediterranean may lie under the usual high-pressure influence, but it is unusually cold there. The northerly winds make it 4°C in Majorca and in Rome only 1°C.

The further development of the weather situation is determined by complicated physical processes not perceptible to either our senses or any measuring equipment at ground level. So in each case we need the support of the big computer centres of the weather services. Their output is in the form of maps transmitted to facsimile receivers.

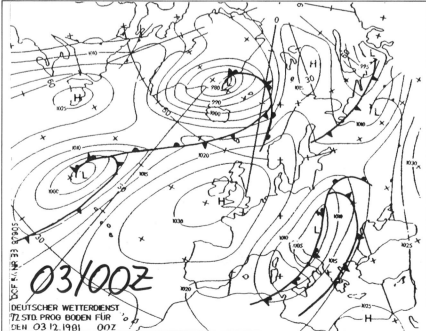

Surface forecast for 0000 on 3.12.

One can't imagine a better basis for passage planning than the forecast maps for three days ahead. The quality of each forecast can easily be checked the next day, by comparing it with the actual conditions.

What conclusions can be drawn from this forecast?

The low over Poland is due to move over the Baltic – entirely contrary to the idea among laymen that depressions in our latitudes move east. For the Baltic this means narrower spacing of the isobars, i.e. more wind. The Atlantic low is due to develop into a fast mover: in 24 hours' time, its core should already lie over Hesse and dominate southern Germany with its rain-fronts.

For Mediterranean sailors this will bring an improvement in the weather, but watch it! True, it is forecast to get milder in the Med. on 1 December, because the wind backs to west and thus relatively warm air from the Biscay area provides some warmth, but you can already see the danger here: the *mistral*. Associated with the low are two cold fronts moving from north to south (in the direction of the arrows on the fronts) in succession. If these get as far as the Med, a *mistral* will blow. Starting from such a peaceful situation, the forecast map thus provides long

enough warning to avoid making long open-sea passages if you don't want to be knocked about. If, a little later, you map the surface forecast for the 2nd and 3rd, you will find this implicit warning impressively confirmed.

How a surface analysis map is worked out

1. Check that date and time are *clearly* legible, otherwise draw them on boldly.
2. Hatch the land masses to improve legibility.
3. Overwrite the pressure centres with a large red L in each depression centre and a large blue H for the highs.
4. Colour over the fronts: warm red, cold blue. Occlusions should be purple, but if you don't have that just use blue over red.
5. Marking thunderstorms: look through the stations (at least those in the vicinity) to see if there have been any thunderstorms. If so, the station is clearly marked with a thunderstorm bent arrow in red.
6. Rain/shower areas: all stations which have reported showers have a shower symbol in green painted over them. Where rain is reported, the station (with its whole report) is overpainted in green. This way you end up being able to see the important bad-weather zones clearly.
7. Fog at any station is marked by yellow.

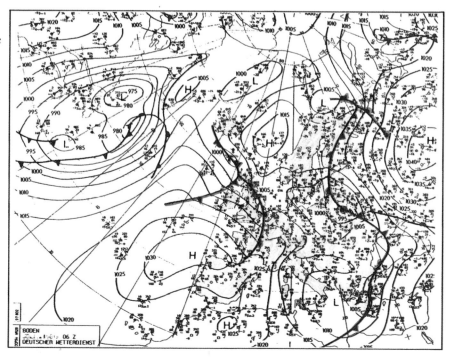

Yet again the weather situation on 30.11., but this time coloured in and thereby made clearer and easier to read.

Over northern Italy, a real storm has developed out of the second cold front, creating a classic *mistral* situation. It doesn't look any better in the other sea areas of the Mediterranean: the storm is raging everywhere although apparently it developed out of nothing.

Finally a warning that cannot be given often enough. Skippers are for ever puzzled when after one forecast the next one says something totally different from what was forecast only 12 hours ago.

The explanation is quite simple. The correct, i.e. the best, forecast map is always the latest one: it automatically invalidates previous maps. That substantial changes in the forecast situation can indeed arise in the course of a few hours is explained quite simply by the fact that in the meantime the meteorologists as well as their computer have acquired more and more recent data on the physical processes going on in the atmosphere. The earlier values, which required revision, were simply not representative enough for an

adequate indication of the true development of the situation. Even in the age of superelectronics, that is something we have to live with.

Which weather maps does one need on board?

From the extensive list offered to the fax-receiver by every weather service, only a certain proportion is of use to the amateur: the rest are special maps for aviation or purely intended for other meteorologists.

These are the maps with which you should work
Surface analysis Europe/North Atlantic
Surface map with station entries
Surface forecast for 24, 48, 72 hours.

These maps are informative and helpful
Map of water temperatures
Sea state analysis and forecast
European station max. and min. temperatures.

Which transmitting station for which sea area?
It is not at all a good idea to continue using the familiar station for as long as possible. The same applies to weather maps as to spoken shipping bulletins: the best station is almost always the nearest one. Of course, to begin with receiving now one station and now another takes a bit of getting accustomed to because they all have different map formats.

Some tips about European fax-transmitters, from practical experience

Offenbach
Transmits around the clock, almost continuously. Map format and legibility good, very punctual. Reception difficulty frequent in the Channel and coastal region of southern France/northern Italy. Transmits only on long wave. A long receiving aerial is important. Isobar spacing 5 mb.

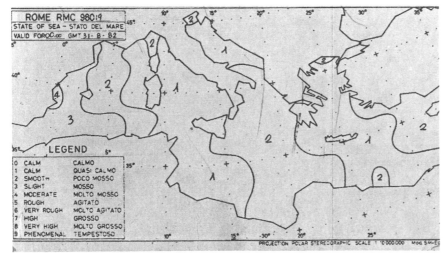

Sea motion analysis map from Radio Rome

A map like this can also be useful when planning a passage. The figures indicate sea state. While in many parts of the Med it is almost calm (1), there is more sea in the western corner. Off the east coast of Spain, north of Denia/Alicante, it's pretty unpleasant (4) for small yachts.

114

Bracknell

Transmits powerfully in a convenient frequency range, best frequency 8040 kHz. Can usually still be received clearly in the North Sea and the Baltic when everything else has 'closed down'. Punctual, high quality forecasts for sea areas around the British Isles and particularly the Atlantic. Analysis and forecast for sea-motion is divided into sea and swell. Isobar spacing 4 mb.

Rota

The Rota transmitter belongs to the U.S. Navy and is located near Cadiz in southern Spain. Surface maps do not show fronts, isobar spacing 4 mb. Long range: the transmitter is aimed at the Atlantic; output into the Med is low.

Paris

Transmits on short wave every 3 hours. Best transmitter for western Med. Both bands have a long range. Good forecasts for the Atlantic. Most important map is surface map with stations, scale 1 : 5 million: has all station reports from the entire Med. coast. Forecast map format requires a bit of getting used to: high = A, low = D.

Monsanto (Lisbon)

Good forecasts for the Iberian peninsula west coast: though deserves to be called erratic: transmission times are interpreted generously.

Madrid

Very good for the coastal waters; for the western Med distinctly improved. High = A, low = B.

Rome

Forecast quality praiseworthy, particularly for western Med. Punctual, good sea state maps.

Belgrade

Unbeaten for the Adriatic and the Ligurian Sea: no better forecasts exist for this region. Good reception, adequate range. No use for other sea areas of the Mediterranean. Transmission times are adhered to. Interference close to coast: change over to Rome.

Quickborn

Like a special transmitter of the German weather service, to supply German ships at sea with serviceable weather maps. The maps transmitted are a selection for normal users, partially taken directly from other weather services, e.g. Moscow, Bracknell.

Advantages: only transmits the sort of maps everyone can understand; important maps are repeated. Warnings to Mariners are transmitted in plain language at fixed times. Good reception also in the Med. Disadvantages: frequently poor reception in North Sea and Baltic, if too close to the transmitter.

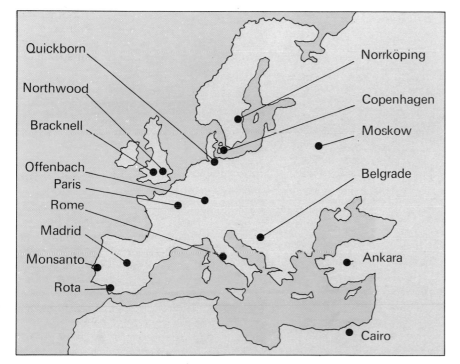

Stations transmitting weather maps

Weather in the North Sea and British Waters

Wind conditions and incidence of gales in summer

Although the North Sea is a relatively small sea and lies in the changeable westerlies zone, one has to make distinctions between its different areas because the mean wind force increases significantly from southeast to northwest. Only the east coast of Britain does not fit into this pattern, because the English/Scottish mountain ranges effectively screen off the prevailing westerly winds. Mean wind force in summer is 3–4. The month with least wind in the German Bight is May. During the summer, about two-thirds of all the winds in the coastal regions are between force 1 and 3. In the open North Sea the proportion of wind in that range reduces to about 50%. Strikingly, the wind strength near the coast is highly variable, by reason of the pronounced character of the land edge. In midsummer the sea breeze is a pronounced feature and may reach force 4. From the table of gale-force days you can see clearly that May and June are quietest; unfortunately

Number of days with gales in the North Sea (March–October)			
Force 8 and over			
Stations	Borkum-Riff LV	Elbe 1 LV	Horns Rev LV
March	2.5	2	1
April	1	1	1.5
May	0–0.5	0–0.5	0
June	0–0.5	0–0.5	0–0.5
July	1	1	0–0.5
August	1	1.5	1
September	2.5	1.5	2.5
October	4	3	4

Number of days with strong winds in the North Sea (March–October)			
Force 6 or more, force 6 having been reached at least once for 10 min. or more. The actual strong wind proportion in May amounts to no more than 5% of the total hours in the month.			
Stations	Borkum-Riff LV	German Bight LV	Elbe 1 LV
March	12.5	16	14
April	9.5	10.5	11
May	8	9	8.5
June	8.5	9	8
July	9	9.5	9.5
August	10.5	12	12
September	12.5	11.5	11
October	16	18	16.5

the water then is still cold. August is the month when you may expect the first summer gale. The second table conveys the same message: May and June are the most peaceful, July represents a transition. Most gales last about half a day, rarely longer than a whole day. When evaluating local reports from the shipping bulletin, you should take account of the following peculiarities.

List (Sylt)

Winds from W to NW are often noticeably higher than reported from other stations, because of the exposed position of the anemometer, which is on top of a dune. The List readings may be considered roughly representative of open-sea conditions; for the inner German Bight subtract one force.

Heligoland

Wind from W around to N is rated far too low because the instrument is sheltered. Particularly following fronts there is considerable damping of the gusts – so watch out!

Elbe 1 Lightship

A very sound adviser whose readings are important for the inner German Bight.

Borkum-Riff Lightship

Winds from W to NW are usually reported at one force higher than at Elbe 1, because it lies in a region where the long fetch can take full effect.

If you have to decide whether to sail

or not, take the following stations as representative:

Winds from W to NW:
  Lightship (LV) German Bight
  LV Borkum-Riff
  LV Elbe 1
  List (Sylt)
Winds from SW to S:
  LV Elbe 1
  LV Borkum-Riff (winds from SW only)
Winds from SE to NE:
  Heligoland
  LV Elbe 1
  LV Borkum-Riff (not for winds from SE)
  LV German Bight
Winds from N:
  List (Sylt)
  LV German Bight
  LV Borkum-Riff
  LV Elbe 1

A personal visit to the weather station is something I can recommend. Even if there are no professional meteorologists who can give you official advice, the people who work with them do have some experience – and a lot more information than a skipper.

Weather stations on the German North Sea coast

Emden, Nesserland lock, tel. (0)4921/21458
Bremerhaven, by the New Lock, tel. (0)471/72220
Cuxhaven, 'Bei der alten Liebe', tel. (0)4721/36400
Heligoland, Harbourmaster's office, tel. (0)4725/606

Number of foggy days in the harbours on the North Sea				
	Emden	Wilhelms-haven	Bremer-haven	Hamburg
March	5	5	9.5	5.5
April	1.5	3	4	2.5
May	0.5–1	1–2	1–2	1.0
June	0–0.5	1	1	0–0.5
July	1.5	1	1	1
August	2	1	3	1.5
September	3	2–3	4–5	4–5
October	5	5	7	7

Foggy days at sea							
Sea area	April	May	June	July	Aug.	Sept.	Oct.
LS Borkum Riff	5	3.5	2.5	1	1	1.5	2.5
LS Weser	5	4.5	2.0	1.5	1.5	2	4
LS Elbe 1	5	4.5	1.5	1.5	0.7	1.5	2.5
LS Horns Rev	5	6.5	4.0	2.0	1	1	1

Fog-prone conditions in the summer half of the year

Fog can occur in the North Sea at any time of the year. Winds involving the highest risk of fog are:

in spring	SW – NW
in summer	W – N
in the autumn	SW – SE

By no means does fog only occur when it's calm: it has been observed with up to force 6. In the North Sea fog occurs mostly at night and disperses after sunrise. Average duration is only 3 hours. Even in the open sea it doesn't last long, and often takes the form of drifting fog-banks.

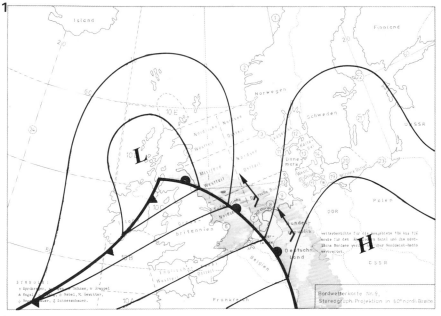

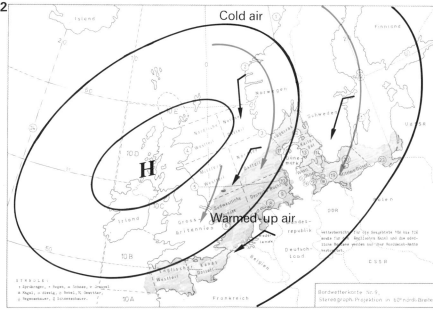

1. Typical fog-prone conditions for spring and early summer

When the water is still significantly colder than the air, warm fronts bring fog. Ahead of the front, warm and moist air is brought down onto the water. The result is fog, which disperses slowly only once the front has passed. Thence also the designation 'warm front fog'.

2. Typical fog conditions for late summer and autumn

If polar air is slowly transported south over the still relatively warm water in the North Sea and the Baltic it warms up in a shallow surface layer and takes up moisture. Under a stable high-pressure influence that moisture cannot be carried away, resulting in persistent fog which does not disperse until that influence is reduced.

Typical fog weather

In spring fog occurs at sea when very warm, and thus also moist, air from southern latitudes is channelled over the still cool North Sea water. Over the Continent there is either only early morning fog or visibility is totally unaffected. But barely has the cold water started to act on the subtropical air mass before the moisture condenses as fog. Unless the weather situation changes, the fog will stay.

In summer, fog is relatively rare. Cold, dry Arctic air warmed slowly and steadily on its way south by warmer sea water takes up a lot of moisture evaporating from the surface, but due to the high temperature of both water and air the latter's moisture absorbing capacity is high. Fog can only occur if the air is cooled drastically below the temperature of the water, as is possible near the coast.

Northerly weather with little wind has the potential to bring fog, because with a clear sky the land cools down overnight so much that the temperature drops below that of the water. The result is thick coastal fog which to seaward often ends just offshore; out at sea the visibility is perfect. Fog at sea in the autumn is rare since the sea water is still warm; autumn fog must be expected increasingly along the coast and in inland regions.

Dense fog in port, which has completely swallowed the sun.

As soon as the fog-blanket tears a bit and you can see the sun distinctly, visibility improves rapidly. Within the hour the fog will have vanished.

You will often find that in harbour there is thick fog, and listening to the station reports in the shipping bulletin the visibility goes up and down all the time. It's 'thickers' at one station; another has 'visibility good'. The explanation lies in the strongly varying water temperatures in the German Bight. Jumps of 2° to 3°C over the shortest of distances are quite usual here. Also known are so-called 'cold eggs', islands of cold water that generate drifting fog banks. Precisely because of the strongly varying and shifting water temperatures, visibility in the seas around Heligoland varies greatly. Naturally, forecasting is correspondingly difficult and must be treated with caution.

Heligoland fog
In late summer/early autumn one frequently observes that towards sunset the island becomes enveloped

Heligoland fog

Initially, the island wraps itself almost unnoticed in mist. It won't be long, though, before it disappears totally in fog.

in a thick haze or even fog. In pronounced high-pressure conditions mist forms initially; anyone approaching the island has got to get within 2 to 3 miles of it to see anything. And then suddenly everything has closed down. Within a few minutes the island is enveloped in thick fog and all that remains is a suggestion of the towers on the upper part. A few hours later the spook is all over. The cause of this sudden fog is cold water, coming in with the flooding tide. A water temperature just one degree lower triggers the fog, which barely extends a mile out.

Anyone without radar or RDF had best creep up to the Dune from the east or southeast; the last half mile is then quite easy, homing in on the foghorn on the south harbour mole. Those who consider that too chancy should anchor in good holding ground east of the Dune until the tide changes and the visibility gets better again.

Thick fog develops suddenly
If surprised in the middle of a busy shipping lane by suddenly developing fog, what one would really like to do is wave a wand and be somewhere else – unless the yacht has radar. Such suddenly appearing fog is called **advection fog**. It is an example of the bringing-in (advection) of very muggy subtropical air, which cools down and contracts over colder water and allows its stored water vapour to condense out. Within a few minutes you are in the thickest pea-souper you can imagine. This is a good place to mention something not everyone knows: not only is the visibility reduced drastically, but also one's ability to judge distance. Objects visible are in reality much closer than they seem. Our eyes make this mistake without telling us!

1

2

Optical illusion in fog

1. The tanker appearing here still seems to be quite a long way off because she has only just been sighted. One's inclination is to feeling quite safe in crossing her bows. Engine noise, strongly damped by the fog, cannot be heard: another reason for considering the ship to be a long way off and/or travelling slowly. Any bow-wave is concealed by the prevailing fog.
2. The result you can see in this picture, taken only a very short time after the first one. A collision threatens and can now only be averted with difficulty.

Using VHF-radio to help you in fog
No matter whether you are in the
North Sea, the Mediterranean, the
Bay of Biscay or the Baltic when fog
takes you by surprise, you are by no
means helplessly exposed to chance if
you have a VHF telephone on board.
Send out a call on Channel 16,
something like*: 'All ships, all ships,
this is sailboat (name, callsign), my
position is 20 nm west of research
platform *North Sea*, my course 350°.

Sailing without radar, all ships in the
vicinity are requested to keep sharp
look-out.' If you don't get any
answer to that, you can breathe more
freely for a start – but repeat the
message every half hour. If a ship
does receive you, not only is he able
to tell you about the traffic in the
vicinity that he can see on his radar,
he'll be happy to give you your exact
position.

Thunderstorms and waterspouts

In northwest Europe thunderstorms
occur almost exclusively in the
summer half of the year. Between
May and September we have 2 to 3
days per month with thunderstorms.
Over the open sea, thunderstorms are
distinctly less frequent than in the
coastal region and over land. The

*Correct message as follows
'Sécuritée, sécuritée, sécuritée all
ships, all ships, all ships, this is (ship's
name 3 times, callsign), sécuritée
(ship's name, callsign). Approximate
position . . . degrees . . . minutes North,
. . . degrees . . . minutes East (West)
proceeding under sail in dense fog,
heading . . . degrees, speed . . . knots. No
radar equipment on board, all ships are
requested to keep sharp lookout and
indicate. This is (ship's name, callsign), over'.*

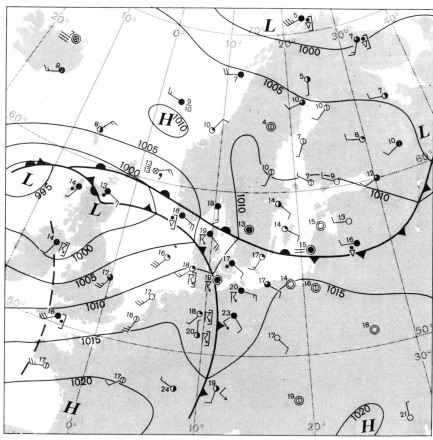

**Typical summertime southerlies conditions with thun-
derstorms along the cold front.**

U.K. Radio Weather Information

Station	kHz	Frequency Metres	MHz	Times GMT or BST
BBC Radio 4	**198**	**1515**		**0033, 0555, 1355, 1750, 0038**
BBC Radio 3	1215	247		0655
BBC G. London	1458	206	94.9	Shortly before or after hr. 0700–2400
Essex Radio	1431	210	96.3	Mon–Fri: 0630, 0730, 0830
	1359	220	102.6	Sat–Sun: Hr. + 05, 0600–1200
BBC Radio Kent	1035	290	96.7	Mon–Fri: 0645, 0745, 0845, 1708, 1808
	1602	187		Sat: 0645, 0745, 0845, 0945, 1300
	774	338	104.2	Sun: 0745, 0845, 0945, 1300
BBC Radio Sussex	1485	202	95.3	Mon–Fri: 0600, 0630, 0700, 0730, 0800, 0830 then on hr.
	1161	258	104.5	Sat: hourly except 12.00 and 1700
	1368	219	104	Sun: hourly till noon
BBC Radio Solent	999	300	96.1	Mon–Fri: 0633, 0733, 0745, 0833, 1733, 2300
	1359	221		Sat: 0633, 0733, 0745, 0833, 1925
				Sun: 0633, 0733, 0745, 0904, 1504
BBC Radio Devon	990	303	95.8	Mon–Fri: 0605, 0632, 0732, 0832, 1310, 1732
	885	351	103.4	Sat: 0600, 0632, 0732, 0832, 1310
	801	375	94.8	Sun: 0830, 1310
	1458	206	103.4	
BBC Radio Cornwall	657	457	95.2	Mon–Fri: 0628, 0715, 0745, 0815, 1245, 1645
	630	476	103.9	Sat: 0720, 0745, 0845, 0915, 1100
			96.0	Sun: 0745, 0845, 1300
BBC Radio Bristol	1548	194	95.5	Mon–Fri: 0604, 0632, 0659, 0707, 0732, 0759, 0807, 0832, 0858, 0904,
			94.9	1004, 1104, 1204, 1233, 1259, 1307, 1404, 1504, 1604, 1632, 1704, 1750,
			104.6	1804
				Sat: 0704, 0804, 0830, 0904, 1004, 1204, 1304
				Sun: 0704, 0804, 0904, 1004, 1204, 1304
BBC Radio Merseyside	1485	202	95.8	Mon–Fri: 0633, 0733, 1145, 1309, 1804
				Sat: 0735, 0935, 1304, 1804
				Sun: 0904, 1404, 1804
Radio Clyde	1152	261	102.5	0605, 0705, 0805, 0915, 1630
North Sound Radio	1035	290	96.9	0600, 0715, 0745, 0815 – then hourly till 1715, 1815.
				Sat–Sun: 0900, 1000, 1200, 1300, 1400
Radio Forth	1548	194	97.3	Hourly
BBC Radio Newcastle	1458	206	95.4	Mon–Fri: 0655, 0755, 0855, 1155, 1655, 1755
			96.0	
			104.4	Sat–Sun: 0755, 0855, 0955, 1150
BBC Radio Humberside	1485		95.9	Mon–Fri: 0632, 0732, 0832, 1632, 1730
				Sat–Sun: 0730, 0830
BBC Radio Norfolk	873	344	104.4	Mon–Fri: 0610, 0710, 0810, 0850, 1310, 1710
	855	351	95.1	Sat–Sun: 0700, 0800, 0900, 1000, 1100, 1300, 1400
BBC Radio Jersey	1026	292	88.8	Mon–Fri: 0710, 0732, 0815, 0828, 0904, 1315, 1402, 1740
				Sat: 0805, 0815, 0830, 0900
				Sun: 0730, 0802, 0815, 0830, 0910, 1158

summer heat thunderstorms, if they occur at all over the sea, don't start before the second half of the night and don't last long.

There is a need for care if front thunderstorms should turn up; for this to happen, there are two typical weather situations.

Summer

If there is a depression over the British Isles and the northern North Sea, it often results in a major air-mass contrast in the region of the front. In the warm sector, the low draws in muggy subtropical air from the south; behind the cold front there is an inflow of pretty cold and dry polar air. These are the most favourable conditions for fierce front thunderstorms, accompanied by pronounced line-squalls.

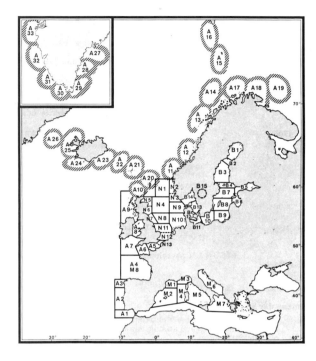

Overseas Radio Weather Services in English			
Country/station	Frequency kHz	Times GMT	Forecast Area
Denmark Ronne	2586, Ch. 4	On request	North Sea & Danish coastal waters
Skagen	1701	On request	North Sea & Danish coastal waters
Norway Bergen	416 1743, Ch. 02, 05, 21, 24, 25, 64, 85, 87	On request	Coastal waters of W. Norway
Germany Norddeich	474	On request, 0800, 2000	German Bight
	2614	0810, 2010	German Bight
Holland Scheveningen	421	0930, 1530, 2130	North Sea (See map page 126)
	1862	0340, 0940, 1540, 2140	
	1890	0304, 0940, 1540, 2140	
Belgium, Ostende	435, Ch. 27	0820, 1720	Belgian coast, Dover, Thames

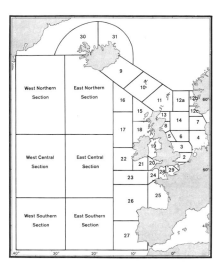

Autumn

The water in the North Sea is still fairly warm and acts as a hotplate for the air mass above it. During northerlies, which carry a tall bank of cold air towards the Continent, the atmosphere becomes very unstable. At high level it is very cold, and the layer next the sea is warmed by the water: the result is numerous heavy showers around thunderstorms.

Waterspouts occur almost exclusively in late summer, always in association with a break-in of cold air.

Shipping bulletins for the North Sea

Reed's Nautical Almanac, the *Macmillan & Silk Cut Nautical Almanac*, the Admiralty *List of Radio Signals*, and publications of other national weather and maritime authorities all give times, frequencies and languages of stations in the British Isles and on the Continent that transmit weather information. Only a selection of sources can be listed here, and readers should remember that details may change.

1	Dover	16	Bailey
2	Thames	17	Rockall
3	Humber	18	Malin
4	German Bight	19	Irish Sea
		20	Lundy
5	Tyne	21	Fastnet
6	Dogger	22	Shannon
7	Fisher	23	Sole
8	Forth	24	Plymouth
9	Southeast Iceland	25	Biscay
		26	Finisterre
10	Faeröes	27	Trafalgar
11	Fair Isle	28	Portland
12a	Viking	29	Wight
12b	N Utsire	30	Denmark Strait
12c	S Utsire		
13	Cromarty	31	North Iceland
14	Forties		
15	Hebrides		

UK VHF coastal radio stations and times of weather reports		
Station	Channels	Transmission time (GMT)
Niton	4, 28, 81	0833 2033
Jersey	25, 82	0645 1245 1845 2245
Start Point	26	0803 2003
Lands End	27, 88	0803 2003
Severn	25	0833 2033
Anglesey	26	0803 2003
Celtic Radio	24	0833 2033
Portpatrick	27	0833 2033
Clyde	26	0833 2033
Shetland	27	0803 2003
Collafirth	24	0803 2003
Orkney	26	0803 2003
Cromarty	28	0803 2003
Stonehaven	26	0833 2033
Forth	24	0833 2033
Cullercoats	26	0803 2003
Humber	26	0833 2033
Bacton	7	0833 2033
Thames	2	0803 2003
North Foreland	26	0803 2003
Hastings	7	0803 2003

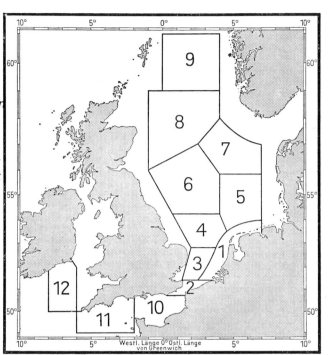

 1 Netherlands
    coastal region
 2 Dover
 3 Thames
 4 Humber
 5 Duitse Bocht
 6 Doggersbank
 7 Vissersbank
 8 Fladen-
    gronden
 9 Vikingbank
10 Kanaal Oost
11 Kanaal West
12 Zuid-Ierland

because of the close proximity of the North Sea.

Weather around Britain

The weather in the waters around the British Isles is better than its reputation. There are two reasons for this: the Azores high and the European extension of the Gulf Stream. The enormous Azores high, which in summer dominates large areas of the North Atlantic, not only extends northwards but also spreads into the Biscay area in the form of a ridge and often determines the course of the weather for the British Isles.

The Gulf Stream plays a significant part in giving the British Isles and their coastal regions a temperature and balanced summer. Coming from North America, it splits in the North Altantic into two branches which flow around the British Isles and warm them. The northern branch extends around the Hebrides, Orkney and Shetland bringing them very mild winters as well as balanced summers. The southern branch favours the green paradise Ireland, the southwest of England, and the English Channel. Along these coasts, the warmest in northwestern Europe, tropical plants grow all the year round. The North Sea coast is not quite so splendidly served: though it is well sheltered from the frequent southwest to west winds, it is nothing like so warm, the temperatures being comparable with Denmark's.

Summer weather in the Scottish region is unsettled. The reason for this lies in the Atlantic weather fronts rapidly passing through, which mostly skim the north. The danger of strong winds is substantially greater

Weather in the Netherlands Region

The weather in the Netherlands differs only a little from that in northern Germany: on average it's a bit better. However the number of days with a flat calm is three times what it is for Heligoland. Between the coast and the islands off it, there are more hours of sunshine than anywhere else on the North Sea. In summer, thunderstorms turn up once a week on average; they are short-duration heat thunderstorms.

Fog can occur at any time in the year. While during the winter half of the year every other day brings fog or poor visibility (haziness) in Dutch

waters, even in summer there is still fog on about one day in ten.

The **sea breeze** is a pronounced feature along the Dutch coast; it gets up to force 3 to 4. In the channels between the islands it usually blows more strongly, whereas the islands have it less often. The waters between the Frisian Islands chain and the coast are thus ideal for small, shallow-draft boats. The best coastal regions for making use of the sea breeze are the strip from den Helder to Europoort, the Schelde, and the coast around Ostend.

There is a good sea breeze circulation along practically the whole of the IJsselmeer shores. The only exception is the western side, where a daily circulation does not develop than in the southern part of the region, but it's a consolation that by virtue of the shelter from the offshore islands there are seldom really heavy seas. The sea lochs and secure bays into which one can sneak are numerous.

Sailors in UK waters enjoy a multitude of sources of information and advice about the weather unequalled anywhere else. Nearly all VHF coastal radio stations routinely carry the weather for their own and adjoining regions at fixed times; about 17 local broadcasting stations carry weather reports for the coast and coastal waters. Last but not least, the Coastguard (call Ch 16) looks after the safety of yachtsmen with a service worthy of note. From any Coastguard station you will receive free of charge weather information for its region, including sea conditions or other local peculiarities. Details are in *Reed's Nautical Almanac* and the *Macmillan and Silk Cut Almanac*: a selection are listed on page 123. The Marinecall telephone weather information service is detailed on page 160.

Overseas Radio Weather Services				
Country/station	Language	Frequency kHz	Times GMT *indicates 1 hr. early when daylight saving time in force	Forecast Area
Denmark Kalundborg	Danish	245, 1062	0450, 0750, 1050, 1650, 2150 Sun: 0645, 2205*	North Sea & Danish coastal waters
Norway N. Broadcasting S.	Norwegian	155, 218, 629, 674, 701, 890, 1313, 1578, 6015	0500, 0600, 0700, 1020, 1100, 1400, 1730, 2100 Sun: 0600, 0800, 1130, 1730, 2100*	N. Atlantic, Eng. Channel, Norwegian coastal waters
Germany Norddeutscher Rundfunk	German	702, 828, 972	Hourly-detailed forceast 2305*	German Bight
Radio Bremen	German	936	0600, 1200, 1800, 2205*	German Bight, central North Sea.
Belgium B. Radio & TV. S.	Dutch	926	0500, 0600, 0700, 0800, 1100, 1200, 1600, 1700, 1800, 2200*	Dover, Thames, Humber, Wight, Portland
France Radio France	French	164, 1071	0555, 1905*	N.E. Altantic Area. Small craft bulletin Mar 15–Oct 31
Boulogne	French	1694 1771 Ch. 23	0703, 1733* Every odd hour + 03 0633, 1133*	North Sea & English Channel
Brest Radio France	French	1071 Ch. 26	0633, 1133*	W. English Channel, N. Biscay

Weather in the Baltic

Wind conditions and incidence of gales

Early summer in the Baltic is characterised by instability of the wind direction. Not until midsummer is there a clearly preferred direction; then westerlies prevail.

Wind strength is at its lowest monthly average in May and June, the direction being variable. The mean for the summer half of the year is force 3. Summer months have 6 to 9 days of calm. In the autumn the prevailing winds are from the south.

Strong winds are a rarity in summer; a mere 7 to 11% of all wind readings for this period gave force 6 or above. Even compared with that, the **frequency of gales** with 1.0 to 1.6% looks very modest. Comparison with the North Sea shows that both seas are affected to about the same extent. For fairly obvious reasons: the first late summer gales mostly arise during pronounced westerly situations when the depressions move east rapidly over both sea areas.

Local wind systems establish themselves in summer in many coastal regions. The sea breeze reaches force 3; the nocturnal land breeze is rarely observed and if it occurs is pretty weak. In early summer the sea breeze affects only a narrow strip of coast; 2 to 3 miles out the sea is like a mill-

Frequency of Baltic gales		
	Average gale frequency in % (force 8 or more)	Strong-wind frequency in % (force 6 or more)
March	2.8	10.8
April	1.6	9.9
May	0.3	6.8
June	1.5	9.4
July	1.0	7.2
August	1.2	10.7
September	1.4	10.6
October	3.1	15.9

pond and there is calm. The cause is the slow warming-up of the water in the Baltic, which often lags behind that in the North Sea. Around this time the shipping bulletin again and again mentions winds of some strength, but out at sea there is still a flat calm. The explanation is simple: the bottom layer of air, some metres thick, is stabilized by the cold water and stays calm. Even as low as at spreader level there may be a noticeable breeze and the anemometer at the masthead turns merrily. At that height the wind is blowing precisely as forecast.

When evaluating station reports from a shipping bulletin, there are some peculiarities of which you should take acount:

Fornaes
With all westerly winds there is a distinct lee effect, one to two wind-force steps less than at sea, so the report is not representative for the Kattegat. With easterly winds, on the other hand, this station report is very good.

Kullen
In westerly winds, the values here are somewhat higher than at sea because the coast with high cliffs baffles the wind. With east wind, a distinct lee-effect lowers speeds.

Kiel lighthouse
This is an automatic weather station, thence the obligatory (and superfluous) message: '...no observation' in the Radio Kiel shipping bulletin.

Fehmarn Belt
A very reliable indicator of wind conditions in the open Baltic.

Arcona, Bornholm, Hel
With wind up to force 4, the reported direction often does not fit in with the run of the isobars on the on-board weather map. Reason: local changes of direction due to the shape of coast and also land or sea breeze.

Ristna
Radio Kiel shipping bulletin often has a report from station Ristna instead of one from weather ship L. Ristna is on Dagö Island in the Gulf of Riga.

Water level variations in the Baltic

Major water level variations in the Baltic are caused by wind-thrust, not tides. Lengthy periods of southwest wind result in the water literally being pushed away from the coast. Particularly in the fjords of Sleswig-Holstein, the depth of water can be reduced substantially: reductions of 1 m or more occur repeatedly in the year. That leaves many a yacht sitting on the putty, and if no one bothers about the boat this can have serious consequences. Don't secure your boat with too little line: if you allow for variations in the water level of ± 0.5 m you will have done well enough for the summer months. The really big variations with extreme

water levels need only be anticipated in late summer and autumn. Persisting northeasterlies raise the level considerably; Travemünde is in the lead here with precisely 2.0 m, but the other fjords are not far behind. We are talking about increases/ reductions in the mean water level, which arise uniformly and are not tied to any bad weather. It is precisely that which causes the risk of this problem being overlooked.

Real storm floods fortunately are rare in the Baltic as with maximum levels of 3 m they flood parts of the coast. Such surges don't occur in summer. The NDR and WDR issue storm-flood warnings if the water rise could exceed 1.5 m.

An interesting and at the same time dangerous phenomenon can often be observed in the Baltic: oscillation of the water, which surges to and fro like water in a rocked bucket. If after a spell of southwest wind the water has drained away pretty thoroughly, it sometimes comes back extremely rapidly and in the harbours and fjords surges to up to 1 m above the average level. That may result in a total water level variation of 2 to 3 m in one day. Such rapid changes have to be reckoned with particularly if the wind turns easterly after low water. This surging is only slightly less marked if you get a calm after strong southwesterly winds.

Water level variations in the Baltic, in cm				
	Low water		High water	
	maximum	average	maximum	average
Flensubrg	− 147	− 112	+ 175	+ 120
Kiel	− 132	− 99	+ 184	+ 124
Travemünde	− 150	− 115	+ 200	+ 130

Currents in the Baltic

Though with a tidal range of 10 to 20 cm tides in the Baltic can be disregarded, one encounters currents of which some are significant. They are caused other than by tide.

In the Baltic there is a clear relationship between certain weather situations and surface water currents. Because of the complex structure of the coast and the islands, the current in many areas does not set with the wind that is causing it. The highest current velocities are reached at the narrows (Belts, Sound); particularly with east or west winds, the currents here are strong. Average speeds of 1 to 2 knots are usual, but can be exceeded substantially.

Currents when wind is strong

Gedser	average	1.0–1.5 kn
	maximum	3.0–4.0 kn
Fehmarn	average	1.5–2.0 kn
Belt	maximum	4.0–5.0 kn
Open sea	average	0.0–0.5 kn
	maximum	1.0–1.5 kn

Currents when wind is light

Open sea		0.0–0.5 kn
Gedser, Fehmarn Belt		1.0–1.5 kn

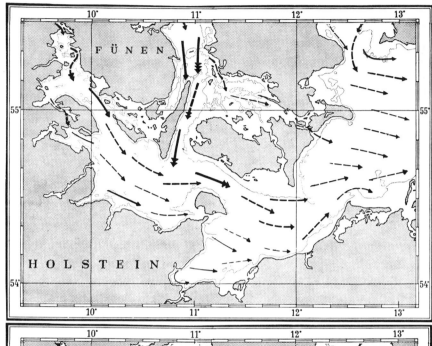

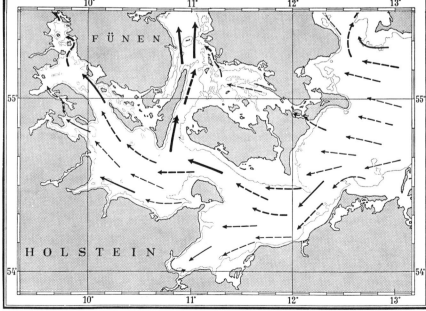

Currents in the Baltic, depending on wind direction
1. Surface currents with strong westerly winds
2. Surface currents with strong easterly winds

Weather situations producing strong currents

Westerlies
The fast flowing currents in the Baltic are caused by marked westerlies, when you get two forces co-operating. The wind literally pushes the water eastwards, creating a current in the Gedser Strait and the Fehmarn Belt. The drop in the level in Kiel Bay then results in a follow-up flow from the Belts, which furthermore is substantially reinforced by pressure from the waters in the Skagerrak, being powerfully driven into the Kattegat by the westerlies.

Long-lasting westerlies thus cause all the individual factors in the Baltic region to act in concert and so produce unusually fast-flowing currents, to the confusion of many a sailor. Particularly in the narrows of the Belts, there can be currents against which it is not easy to make headway even with a favourable wind (e.g. Middelfahrt, Faeno).

Easterlies
Marked easterlies produce a build up of water in Kiel Bay, which then causes a current in the open sea, up to 1 knot in the direction of the wind. The accumulated water drains slowly through the Belts which thus get a north-flowing current. If the east wind lasts for more than a day, current speeds in the narrows can easily reach 4 to 5 knots – the sort of values which simply must be taken into account when planning a passage. Anyone planning to sail through the Great Belt towards Kiel with a moderate wind, for instance, had better prepare for a lengthy passage: making good distance over the ground will not be easy. The same applies to going northwards in a marked westerly.

Northerlies and southerlies
Though in these situations the Belts behave like corridors through which the wind is funnelled, only slower currents result. Even strong southerlies rarely cause currents flowing faster than 1 to $1\frac{1}{2}$ knots in the direction of the wind; north wind currents are weaker still.

Fog conditions

Overall it can be said that the Baltic, and particularly the western part, averaged over the year has good visibility. In the transitional spring and autumn months it's merely the coastal regions where the visibility is somewhat restricted. In summer the days with fog add up to less than 1% Visibility reduced by haze, at 5% of all the days, also does not amount to anything significant.

Typical fog weather
A powerful and stable high over southern Sweden and the Baltic, in combination with light winds, is inclined to generate early morning coastal fog. It disperses rapidly during the forenoon: average duration is 5 to 6 hours. During the day the weather in all sea and coastal areas is fair and visibility good.

Thunderstorms and waterspouts

It's not that thunderstorms are a rarity in the Baltic, but with an incidence of 15 to 20 days per year it is what you might call the least thunderstormy region of our European sailing waters. Summer months show 2 to 4 days with thunderstorms.

Days of fog in the Baltic			
	Sonderburg	LS Fehmarn Belt	Bornholm
March	4	8.5	6
April	2	4.5	6
May	0.3	3.2	5
June	0.3	1.0	2
July	0.5	0.9	2
August	1	0.7	1
September	2	1.5	2
October	3	3.2	3

Frequency of thunderstorms in the Baltic		
	German Baltic coast	Bornholm
March	0.2	0
April	0.7	0.3
May	2.1	0.9
June	3.1	1
July	3.9	2
August	3.2	2
September	1.2	1
October	0.2	0.3

A typical weather development is responsible for the few that do occur: if after a settled period of high pressure a cold front crosses the Baltic, you have to reckon with thunderstorms. On top of that there are some supplementary factors which allow an even closer assessment of the probability of thunderstorm-activity.

Initial situation

A stable high over the Continent and Scandinavia, with predominantly gentle southeast winds, has generated pretty dry warm air over the Baltic and the coastal region. A cold front brings moist and moderately warm sea air in over the sea from the west. The cold front must move eastwards quickly to retain the clear contrasts between the air masses. That is usually when thunderstorms occur in the warm air, well ahead of the cold front. There is a high risk of water-spouts, even ahead of the thundery front. Should you see heavy cumulus building up as part of this development, there is a risk of thunderstorms, even if a friendly sun is still shining through the cloud. The barometer scarcely gives positive advice in this situation; the pressure drop is small and vague. Better to rely on the crackling and interference on medium wave radio. At the latest, when the cumulus has closed over, there will be a deceptive calm, it will become hazy and the clouds will turn an orangy-yellow. Should these signs occur it's high time you had the boat secured for rough weather. The thunderstorms do arrive like 'a bolt from the blue', and with gale-force gusts. They ease up quickly behind the cold front, but watch out for reference to a 'following trough' in the shipping bulletin. That would mean strong winds, and again thunderstorms, the next day. Usually it also means the end of a spell of fine weather.

Typical weather conditions

The Skagerrak Low

This refers to the very rapid establishment of a depression in the Skagerrak, or rather the Oslo Fjord. The precondition for such a development is a northerly air flow towards the Norwegian coast, such as you get when a low has passed from Scotland via the northern North Sea over to central Scandinavia. Polar air masses then flood over the Norwegian highlands, with a build-up at the north coast (windward edge) the south coast and Oslo Fjord becoming leeward zones. There, downwind of such mighty highlands, a depression develops because the air flowing high over the rocky mass draws up that over the water, causing a low on the leeward side of the land. The precondition is encountered quite often during the summer. However, since then the winds are not very strong, the depressions that develop are not very large or deep; quite often they don't show up at all on the weather map. They nevertheless determine the weather in the Skagerrak: if, instead of the 'light to moderate breeze from west to north-west' of the shipping bulletin you find a totally different wind, be it faint and variable in direction or strong, you can be sure that a minor lee-depression has formed and locally is standing the whole forecast on its head. If the barometer, starting in the morning, shows falling atmospheric pressure, and there is no sign of wind from the forecast direction or in the forecast strength, you have a lee-low. Usually these wind systems break down again in the evening, and it

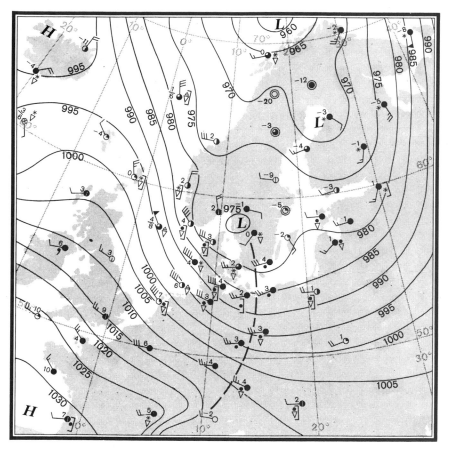

forming in the Skagerrak and the Oslo Fjord, are also the cause of a totally contrary phenomenon in the same sea area: a *föhn*-type clearance. The build-up along the north coast of Norway can lock-in all of the moisture in the air mass, so that after crossing the highlands one finds a cloudless sky. If the flow from the north becomes well established, the whole of the Skagerrak, Kattegat, Jutland, Sleswig-Holstein and its coasts is entirely free of cloud. This cloudless zone extends like a tongue southwards from the Norwegian highlands, so even in late autumn, when in the rest of Germany it is cold and showery, you can still have some lovely days. Sadly this situation only lasts a few days.

Summertime high-pressure gale

At breakfast time you glance at the barometer: a slow and steady rise, so continuing fair weather and a comfortable passage. A look at the sky also promises nothing but good: not a cloud to be seen. Out at sea the situation looks unchanged and the barometer endorses the fond hopes of the crew by continuing to rise. But almost unnoticed the wind strengthens and soon qualifies as 'strong', later even reaching gale force and continuing like that for several days. What has happened? You have chanced into a high-pressure gale, which occurs commonly in summer. The initial situation is always an extensive high whose dominance is now being disputed by a comparatively small low. You are in the middle of this atmospheric conflict, from which the high will be the victor.

Typical development of a storm in the Skagerrak

Particularly in the autumn, the behaviour of the pressure needs watching. If it begins to fall distinctly and rapidly while the wind is dropping, a harmless lee-depression will swiftly deteriorate into a storm-low (pressure drop more than 1 mb per hour).

goes calm. A confident forecast for the Skagerrak low unfortunately is not possible in summer. Things can look quite different the next day, without any change in the weather situation. From late autumn onwards, such a depression can rapidly develop into a proper storm, particularly if a cold front crosses the Norwegian ridge.

The Norway föhn

The same overall weather conditions as are responsible for a depression

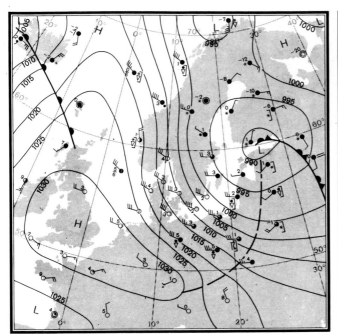

Characteristic weather situation for a Norway föhn.

In this example the whole of Jutland, Sleswig-Holstein and large areas of the Baltic are totally free of cloud. These conditions could also bring a high-pressure gale from the northwest.

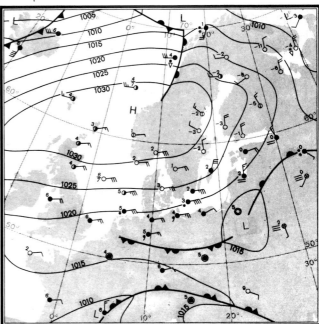

High-pressure gale from the east.

The Kattegat, Belts and Sound are totally free of cloud.

Where there is a stable high-pressure formation centred over the British Isles, the North Sea and Scandinavia, there is a tendency in summer for a shallow depression to form over southern Sweden. One is liable to disregard this somewhat because the high-pressure influence is due to persist – at least according to the forecast. When an extensive high moves, according to the rules it ought to push aside such minor disturbances, or even fill them.

However, it can happen that such small lows withstand the pressure of the high for a few days; what then results is a drastic crowding of the isobars between the two pressure centres.

If you sail into a prolonged pressure rise, check on the weather map where the nearest low is. If the shipping bulletin mentions a low due to move away slowly, the wind must not get any stronger if the weather is to be as forecast. Otherwise, watch

extra carefully to see whether the forecast is actually realized. Rising pressure with increasing wind is a sure sign of a high-pressure gale. If a depression develops over southern Sweden, the gale comes from the northwest. A different situation brings a gale from the east: a low over central Germany and Poland with the high in the same place as before.

Shipping bulletins for the Baltic

An annual summary of all stations transmitting shipping bulletins (*Wetterund Warnfunk*) is issued in leaflet form by the German Hydrographic Institute, Hamburg. *Reed's Nautical Almanac* and the *MacMillan & Silk Cut Almanac* also give all the stations, frequencies and transmission times.

Baltic Radio Weather Services in English			
Country/station	Frequency kHz	Times GMT	Forecast area
Sweden			
Stockholm	416	0900, 2100	The Baltic (See map 1, p. 136)
	518	0730, 1930	
	1771	0933, 2133	
	1778	0933, 2133	
Göteburg	450	0900, 2100	Skaggerak and Kattegat
	1785	1033, 2233	
	Ch. 24, 26, 82	0633, 1433	
Poland			
Gdynia	447	0100, 0700, 1300, 1900	Baltic and Polish coastal
	2726	0135, 0735, 1335, 1935	(See map 2, p. 136)
	Ch. 26		
Denmark			
Ronne	2586, Ch. 4	On request	Danish Coastal Waters
Skagen	1701	On request	Danish Coastal Waters

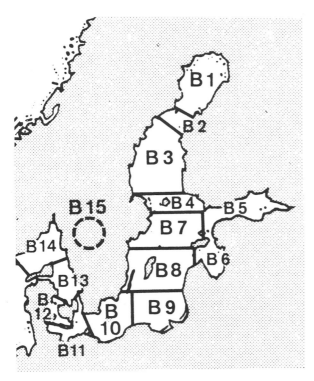

Baltic Key map 1

**Radio Stockholm
forecast areas**

B1 Bottenwiek
B2 Norra Kvarken
B3 Bottenzee
B4 Åland waters and Åland
     islands
B5 Gulf of Finland
B6 Gulf of Riga
B7 Northern Baltic
B8 Central Baltic
B9 Southeastern Baltic
B10 Southern Baltic
B11 Western Baltic
B12 Belts and Sound
B13 Kattegat
B14 Skagerrak
B15 Lake Vänern

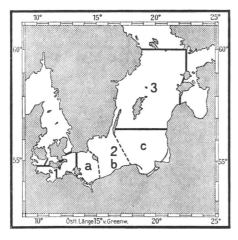

Key map 2

**Radio Gdynia
forecast areas**
1 Western Baltic
2 Southern Baltic
  a) western part
  b) middle part
  c) eastern part
3 Northern Baltic

Weather in the Mediterranean

The principal winds and their occurrence

The Mediterranean is among Europe's most popular sailing regions. With steady light winds and splendid dry summer weather as a basis, sailing is an undiluted pleasure. One is spared gales due to depression formations in summer, although bad weather does occur. Nevertheless the Med is one of Europe's most dangerous sea areas. It does not have any weather ships and merchant ship reports are pretty sparse. That worries the meteorologists, because they absolutely must have information about the weather over the open sea.

Another peculiarity is that most events are localized and may be relatively short term, which means that much of what happens escapes the observation network. But that is by no means all the problem. Generalizing 'in the Med everything is different' – but why?

Take a look at the map: all around the western Mediterranean there are pretty high mountain ranges, with only a few gaps between the rocky

masses through which the wind has to squeeze. Each of these gaps acts like a funnel for the wind to accelerate through. Any air masses that succeed in crossing the mountains drop with unmitigated force down onto the sea. These katabatic winds are much feared, because they can strike abruptly and with hurricane force. Even low hills and small valleys can generate such winds. Indeed, such local weather phenom-

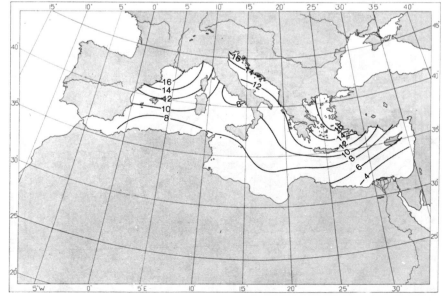

The average annual incidence of winds of force 6 and above, expressed as a percentage. The windiest corners are the Gulf of Lions, the northern Adriatic and the Aegean.

ena play a decisive role in the Med. The powerful solar radiation makes for hot areas of land which coupled with relatively cool areas of water generate local wind systems. The islands, of considerable height, form baffles and thus promote a wind-field substantially independent of the weather map. Exaggerating a little, one can say that every bay and island has its own weather peculiarities.

So in spite of the summer in the Med being on average a season of light winds, heat and dryness, it does have a few surprises for the sailor. Autumn is short and soon turns into winter which has got a kick to it. Although the winter water and air temperatures are perfectly acceptable for North Europeans, the only ones you encounter during this season are a few hardy old salts. The reason: the western Med in winter is the most gale-prone region of Europe. It even beats the North Sea, and gales are twice as frequent as in the dreaded Bay of Biscay. According to the weather statistics, during this season there is a gale every six days. The average wind in February is force 5

or 6. No wonder then that sailing is restricted to the summer.

In spring, when the water reaches its lowest temperature of around 12° to 15° it is still pretty windy, but the small temperature difference between water and air means that there is little rain and the sky already has only a few clouds.

Summer makes a few false starts before winning through, but in the end the Azores high does move north and pushes the Atlantic low formations way up into the Arctic Sea. A ridge advances across Spain towards the Alps, and the Eurasian high usually has disappeared by April. The annual central heat-low has established itself over Asia and extends to the Bosporus. A similar process is occurring over North Africa, where the long-lasting Sahara low is forming: it's why we get the typical summer weather of the Mediterranean region.

Fine though a barograph is in other waters, in the Med in summer it is little use, and a barometer even less. The differences in atmospheric pressure between high and low are

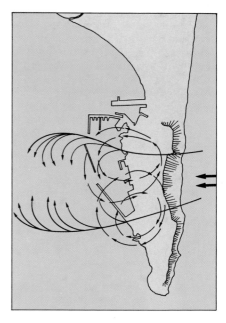

Lee eddies at Gibraltar

These are typical of katabatic winds. Varying with the wind direction, there are some pretty critical patches when approaching Gibraltar harbour in any strong wind blowing from between NE and SE.

The typical summer weather situation for the Med.

Conditions are determined by two pressure centres. The Azores high thrusts out a ridge over Central Europe and the Med. A trough – in this case a heat trough – extends from the Persian Gulf, where a huge heat-low has formed, over the whole of North Africa. In mid-summer the western and the central Med are under high-pressure influence, whereas the eastern Med is influenced by the low and has more wind.

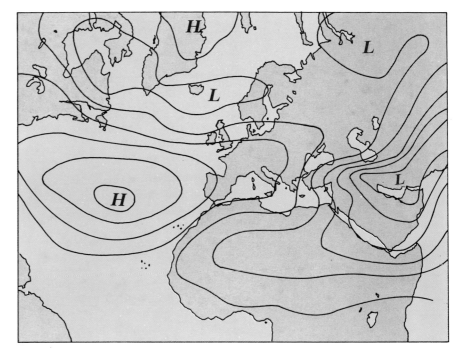

only very small. A depression there does not announce itself with the hefty drop in pressure to which one is accustomed in more northern waters: in the Med it all happens sneakily and usually is only noticed when it's already right overhead. Katabatic winds don't announce themselves: by the time you notice them, your sails are flat on the water. Even such major events as the **mistral** come in without knocking. In March 1977 I was surprised by a hefty *mistral* about 60 n miles south of Toulon. Out of an innocuous weather situation with a 10–15 knot westerly wind, within 20 minutes there had developed a force 10 storm with vicious force 12 hurricane gusts. The waves were 4 to 5 m high and very steep. Apart from wind and waves, the weather was simply glorious – a brilliant, cloudless blue sky and

amazing long-distance visibility: the western Alps gleamed on the horizon. All the while our craft was being tossed about mightily by the *mistral*, the barometer didn't stir, and it hadn't given any warning beforehand either.

A day later, after we had moored off Hyeres, at Sicily's western cape a mean wind speed of 50 knots, a force 10 storm, was being recorded. So for goodness' sake don't think of the *mistral* as only a local phenomenon: after all, Sicily is some thousand kilometres away. Which in a way has already brought us to the most famous, or rather infamous, winds of the Med. We can't describe them all here, because there are some hundred of them, so we shall only include those that are the most important, and the most dangerous.

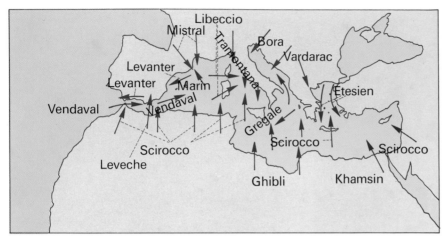

The best-known local wind systems of the Med and their principal directions.

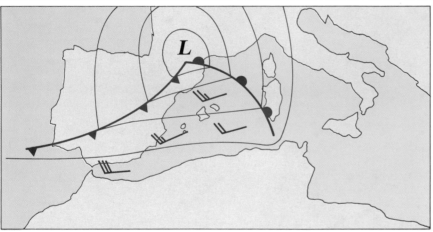

The vendeval

Any low over Spain can bring a vendeval. Together with heavy precipitation there is a pretty hefty wind, strengthening appreciably in the Straits of Gibraltar and extremely gusty.

The levanter

How a gale-force levanter gets up. The more or less permanent Sahara low is in conflict with the ridge from the Azores high. The consequence is crowding of the isobars and hence strong winds or gales.

Vendeval and Levanter

Anyone who has sailed south to the Med by the outside, Atlantic route will have noticed how without apparent reason the wind increases significantly in the approaches to the Straits of Gibraltar and usually then drops again just as quickly in the Alboran Channel. The cause of this is the funnelling effect on the wind as it is forced through between the African Atlas mountains and the Spanish highlands. If the weather map shows southwest to west wind for sea areas Alboran and Nelson, you can confidently add 2 or 3 to the wind force to arrive at its strength in the Straits. If it's whistling in from the west, the locals call it **vendeval**; if blowing from the east, **levanter**. You may have the luck (!) to enounter one of these winds at the front door to the Med at any time of the year, but they are particularly unpleasant in winter because then they get

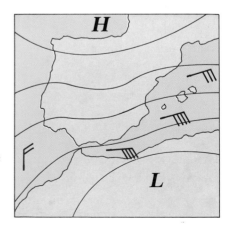

140

The scirocco

Lows passing eastward, or northeastward, across the Med often bring on the scirocco. As the low moves away, the hot desert wind is replaced by the cold air behind it. A scirocco brings hot-and-cold baths.

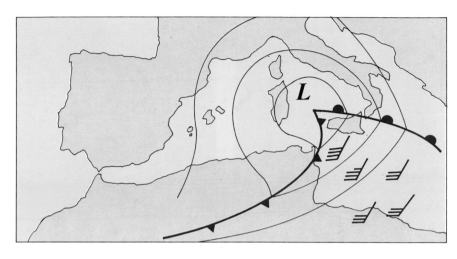

extremely gusty at Gibraltar. It's quite easy to spend a whole day tacking valiantly and at the end of it still to be in the same place. The cause is a surface current which always runs from west to east and is encountered most of the time. If in addition a westerly wind is blowing towards the Straits, its thrust reinforces that current.

If an Atlantic low is approaching Spain, you must always reckon with a *vendeval* in the western Med, often associated with heavy rain and thunderstorms. An uncomfortable high, steep sea builds up quickly. In combination with force 5 to 7 winds, it rapidly puts an end to sailing for pleasure.

Scirocco

This is an unpleasantly hot wind originating in North Africa and blowing from the SW–SE quadrant. In Morocco, Algeria and Tunisia it is called the **chili**. It brings a dry, dusty

heat, sometimes with a sandstorm so strong that the sun is blacked out. However that's rare on the high seas. If on the southern horizon you see a yellow to reddish strip of haze or cloud, there is a *chili* not far off. It generally blows with force 4 to 6, rarely rising.

An unpleasant feature of the *chili* is the temperature fluctuations that accompany it. Abrupt temperature rises of up to 20° are normal. In coastal regions you then get the usual föhn-symptoms. Stress for heart and circulation; one feels listless and easily loses concentration, and becomes irritable. On the high seas it also is uncomfortably to intolerably sticky – because over water the dry desert air rapidly takes up moisture. In the Balearic Islands (Balearics), when there is a scirocco the air is often so humid that the roads are wet as though from rain.

If a large depression over North Africa is due to move north, you can always count on a scirocco. Ahead of such lows, extremely hot Sahara air is then transported into the Mediter-

ranean. If the low rapidly departs eastwards, the heatwave only lasts from a half- to a whole day; pretty cold air then follows in behind the depression. If the Sahara-low is slow-moving, the scirocco can easily last several days; usually it then 'goes to sleep' in the evening. On average the scirocco blows on five days in the month.

Along Spain's southeast coast, up as far as Alicante, there blows a 'dry *scirocco*' called **leveche**. Because of its short journey over water, the wind stays hot and dry. It blows pretty gustily and reaches force 5–7, sometimes even force 8. The further the *scirocco* advances northwards over the Med, the more humid it gets. In the eastern Med in summer it is really pretty rare, occurring on only one to two days a month. Visibility then reduces drastically when the heatwave arrives. A cooling-off period follows, after which the cold air can of course bestow a good deal of wind on you: hurricane-like gusts are very probable for some hours. The *scirocco* is called **samum** in

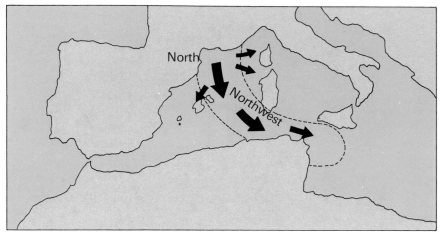

North

Northwest

The mistral 'tongue'

In this region the mistral is strongest. Usually it is sharply focused and reaches the highest speeds in the centre of the tongue. Note its differing directions in the different sea areas: around the Balearics it blows from north to northeast, around Corsica and in northern Sardinia from the west. Out at sea, the principal direction is from the northwest.

Arabia, **ghibli** in Libya and **khamsin** in Egypt.

Mistral

The widely-used name *mistral* covers a multitude of cold-air breakouts in the western Med. When cold air from the Spanish Meseta rushes down the Ebro valley, it is locally called **maestral** or **mestral**. Much better known, and also more feared, is the breakout of Arctic cold air through the Garonne-Carcassone gap, initiated by a cold front advancing towards the Med from the north. No less infamous are the cold-air breakouts from the glacier regions of the western Alps which come roaring down the Rhone valley, all called *mistral*. Usually the dry air brings fine weather – a cloudless sky with splendid long-distance visibility – apart from the wind which strikes with lightning sud-

denness and almost always reaches gale force. Hurricane force with gusts up to 80 knots is no rarity, the greatest danger arising from the primeval force line squalls, which can attain extreme severity. They rush down from the cold highlands onto the sea, and don't give recreational craft a chance. The unexplained loss of yachts of all sizes is attributable to these forces of nature. The danger is greatest between Tortosa and Tarragona, near Perpignan and off the mouth of the Rhone.

The *mistral* changes appearance the farther you get from the coast. The dry air picks up moisture and warms up over the warm sea, producing really miserable weather because now hefty showers and thunderstorms are added to the gale. By no means will it blow from the same direction everywhere: in the Balearics it comes from north to northeast, in the Gulf of Genoa it brings wind from west to southwest. In the Bonifacio and Sicily straits the funnel effect results in a further strengthening of the *mistral*, which there blows from west to northwest.

As regards duration, one can't give any reliable rule. Sometimes it only lasts a few hours, or it can blow for 12 days without any significant break – it can do anything. Close to the coast east of Toulon it doesn't show up heavily; you can be pottering along happily there when farther out it's really blowing (lee effect). A real stinker of a *mistral* is something a sailor or powerboater generally survives only once, if at all. So the trick is to recognize it before things start to hot up.

If a cold front crosses France from the northwest and advances as far as the Med, that guarantees a *mistral*. The faster the front moves and the stronger the wind behind it, the fiercer will the wind be. Come it will, anyway.

The second weather situation which can bring a *mistral* is determined by a low over the Gulf of Genoa or even over northern Italy. The cold air from the Alpine glaciers is pushed downhill. It can't be said too often: even the smallest low over northern Italy, which only just shows a closed isobar, must not be disre-

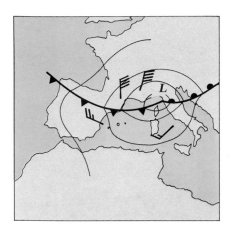

The classic mistral situation

A low has rapidly become established in the Gulf of Genoa. The cold front has crossed France and the cold air behind it drags the air sitting on top of the glaciers down along the Rhone valley to the Med.

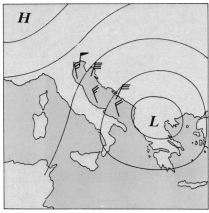

The bora

If a bora dominates the Adriatic, the cause is to be found in either a low over Greece or a powerful high over western Europe.

garded. Such depressions, scarcely visible on the weather map, can within a few hours affect the weather decisively: again, *mistral*.

However the *mistral* can also arrive without any indication on the weather map or in the sky. All of a sudden, the cold glacier air becomes unstuck and tumbles rapidly down-hill. That catches you with your pants down, but things rarely get really hot because these spontaneous line squalls don't last any length of time and are a lot less fierce than they are with a true *mistral*.

Bora

This wind is best known in the northern Adriatic, where it occurs in the form of a breakout of polar air through the gap in the mountain range behind Trieste. In principle the *bora* is no different from the *mistral*: it brings cold, dry air from the mountains onto the sea. The first outbreak of *bora* is often combined with heavy rain or hail; the usual season is late summer to autumn. The moister and warmer the air was which is displaced, the heavier will be the precipitation. Typically, lines of cumulus sit like crests on top of the mountains. If you notice a cloud line like that, the party is about to start: the *bora* is coming silently but swiftly. In the western Adriatic you usually still have a brilliant blue sky, though there is already a decent blow.

When the *bora* lasts longer than one day, it usually arrives in waves. Fierce breakouts of cold air are followed by flat calm, suddenly replaced by wind.

The start of the *bora* is an almighty line squall, which slowly turns into a gale or at least a stiff breeze. The only warning is a very slight drop in pressure beforehand, too late to make your way to a safe haven. Though on the Italian Adriatic coast the *bora* doesn't blow quite so hard, for sailing yachts there is the danger of a lee shore. In making its way across the Adriatic, the *bora* has gradually become a warm, muggy wind which brings heavy showers to that coast.

Most *boras* last up to 12 hours. Longer duration is really known only in the cold season (once over 30 days without a break). According to the statistics, in summer you need to count on a hefty *bora* only once a month, though along the narrowly constricted coastal strip it does occur substantially more often even in summer. In the vicinity of any defile strong katabatic winds can surprise a skipper. The record is held by a gust of 110 knots, measured near Trieste, in winter.

Which are the weather situations that favour the *bora*? Whenever the weather map shows an extensive area over which the wind blows from the north or the northeast, there is a risk. Wind from that direction is usually due to a powerful high over western Europe, or else a low over Greece. If the katabatic wind surprisingly starts to toss your boat about, the thing is to keep your cool: it's happened, so there is no sense in getting excited. Look up to the tops of the mountains to see whether the classic cloud wall is there on the crests. If not, you can be pretty sure that the *bora* will

scarcely last longer than half an hour; all you've got is a local katabatic wind. Just be a bit more careful with the next valley or bay. To avoid the localized downdrafts in the innumerable Yugoslav bays and islands, keep 3 to 5 n miles out to sea.

Gregale

Strong northeast winds in the central Med and around Malta are called *gregale*; it blows predominantly in the cool season and is very similar to the *bora*. It comes from the mountainous regions of Albania and Greece. Only close to the coast is the air cold and dry, out at sea it stays reasonably warm and becomes cloudy and humid.

Around Malta the *gregale* is particularly feared, because due to its long journey over water it can build up waves up to 7 m high. The harbours in the northeast of the island

A threatening line of cloud like this along the crest of the mountains means a bora is imminent.

are then especially exposed. After the wind has died down the swell usually continues for another day or two. As a friendly gesture to sailors, it is very rare in summer: statistically 0.2 days per month.

144

The etesian winds

For them to prevail, the summer low must have become established over the Near East. This is a typical summer situation for the Med.

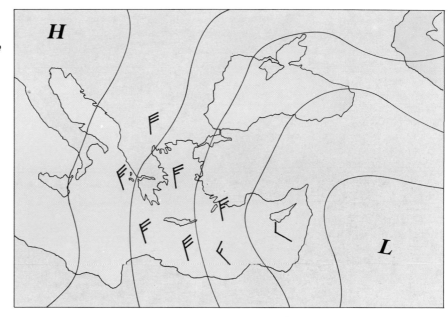

Etesian winds and Meltemi

During the summer the predominant direction of the wind in the Aegean is determined by the extensive heat-low over southwest Asia and Turkey. The wind generated by this is called *meltemi* in Turkish waters, in Greek *etesian*. In the northern Aegean the *meltemi* mostly blows from the northeast; in the central and southern Aegean from the north. In the southern part around Rhodes and near the Turkish coast, it backs more to the northwest.

Since in this area in summer low-pressure formations are pretty rare, the large-scale air current is not disturbed much. That is why the *meltemi* blows so steadily; indeed in some places it even has the character of a trade wind. Quite often it reaches as far as the southern Adriatic and includes the Ionian Sea, where it is similarly reliable and long-lasting. The Greek *etesios* translates into

'annually returning' wind. Every year around the end of May/early June, light northerly winds called *prodroms* (forerunners) get up in the Aegean and Ionian Seas. After they have stopped for a week or two, the summertime northerly *meltemi* and *etesian* winds then start.

On the high seas these winds blow very steadily; only in the vicinity of land are they disturbed by the land/sea breeze circulation. In the northern Aegean the northerly winds bring blue skies and excellent visibility; farther south there is a progressive build-up of cumulus. For the *etesian* winds (*etesian* and *meltemi* are mostly used synonymously) to blow steadily needs a high-pressure region over the Med or southern Europe. So if there is a high here and a low there, you get the *etesian* winds blowing manfully just as expected – force 3–5 is usual.

Caution is called for where the funnel effect may produce a streng-

thening of the wind; there it is quite capable of reaching gale force, and that for many hours. The stretches of water most at risk are the Doro Channel, the waters between the Dodecanese and Turkey, and between Paros and Naxos south to Thira. Near the coast, even the *etesian* winds are subject to a daily cycle: shortly before sunset a calm usually sets in, and next morning the wind starts to blow again.

Libeccio

A wind known along the entire south and west coast of Italy, it blows throughout the year, pretty steadily from the west to southwest. The Ligurian and Tyrrenian Seas are dominated by it. In the Straits of Bonifacio and to the east its strength increases substantially and quite frequently reaches gale force. Along the west coast of Corsica it sets up an unpleasantly choppy sea, and is there also associated with hefty land squalls called *raggiature*.

In summer, in the lee of Corsica (east coast) hot katabatic winds occur almost daily, blowing up to gale force. To steer clear of these when sailing, stay at least 5 n miles from the coast, or 10 to be totally safe from surprises. Between Rapallo and Livorno keep a continuous sharp eye on the *libeccio*, because it sets up a pretty rough sea along the coast of northern Italy.

The impression might have developed that there are scarcely any peaceful days in the Med, with all these katabatic winds and notorious wind systems. But remember that steady light winds and a dry hot summer characterize the weather. Nevertheless it should be said once again: the Med can be dangerous. Because of the gorgeous weather one relaxes one's vigilance and stops being on the alert for the unpleasant surprises which are capable of springing at every corner and almost any time. That is the big danger, not the frequency of events.

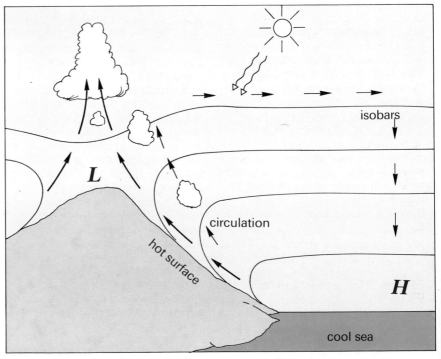

Islands heat up excessively and create their own day-to-day weather

Weather around the islands

The strong sun in the summer months warms the islands intensively so that the layer of air next to the ground gets overheated and rises. Almost every day you get the same sequence: in the morning, a cloudless sky and a flat calm. Towards 9 o'clock at the latest, the first small cumuli form and a light breeze gets up. Until noon the cloud above the island continues to develop; in the later afternoon it collapses again. As the sun sets, so the sea breeze also drops. The well known sea-breeze arrives punctually in the morning and 'goes to sleep' again just as punctually in the evening. For every island you can quite quickly establish from experience when the wind starts in the morning, how strongly it blows, and when it goes down again.

As a rule:
● Small islands don't have a sea breeze, or else only a faint one and it then starts late in the day.
● Large islands have a marked sea breeze that starts early.

Because the sea breeze is a local affair, it doesn't extend out to sea far either; depending on the size of the island, the wind zone is 3 to 5 n miles wide. If you want to sail around the islands and are looking for wind, you therefore need to keep close to the coast.

Recognizing impending worsening of the weather

You can use the familiar sea breeze as a good indirect guide to the threat of worsening weather. We start with the assumption that if the weather is going to continue undisturbed it will continue to follow the rules, i.e. wind and clouds keep to the established daily cycle initiated by the sun's radiation. Any departure of the weather from this pattern indicates a coming change and should be watched carefully.

The sea breeze fails to arrive

In summer, failure of the daily sea breeze to arrive always indicates a change in the weather. There are two possibilities:
● The sea breeze fails to arrive and the atmospheric pressure rises. The weather is going to improve, because all the signs are of an increasing (and probably also fairly long-lasting) high-pressure influence. The increasing pressure (sinking air) prevents the usual formation of swelling cloud, either wholly or partially. A blocking layer (inversion) of the high forms an upward boundary for the clouds. Your morning observation is:
– no sea breeze
– rising atmospheric pressure
– cumulus formation flatter than usual, over land.

● The sea breeze fails to arrive and the atmospheric pressure falls. The weather is going to get worse. Your morning observation is:
– no sea breeze
– slightly falling atmospheric pressure
– cloud thicker than usual.

As a rule, with these symptoms you can expect thunderstorms to build up quickly. Particularly if in the afternoon the cumulus does not collapse but even carries on growing, thunderstorms are a certainty.

Failure of the sea breeze to arrive is always a warning signal, since on a sunny day this can only be due to a compensating wind directly opposing it. This wind will prevail at the latest when the sea breeze dies down. The cause of this 'sea breeze counter-wind' must be a low-pressure formation.

The pressure behaves abnormally

On an undisturbed summer day in the Med you see the barograph drawing neat sine-waves; the atmospheric pressure rises and falls steadily as though with a tidal pattern.
● If the atmospheric pressure deviates from that sine-wave the weather is going to change.

In fact the air-shell of the earth is subject to ebbing and flooding just like the seas and oceans.

You have learnt that this air-shell is incredibly heavy, and the forces of sun and moon also act on it periodically. The atmospheric tide each day ebbs twice and floods twice. 'Low water' is at 10 in the morning and 10 in the evening; 'high water' at 4 in the afternoon and 4 in the morning. The tidal range does depend on the latitude: it increases continuously from Pole to Equator, starting with nil at the Pole and attaining at least ± 5 mb in the Equatorial region. In the Med the range will be about ± 1.5 mb.

If the pressure goes up and down steadily, the weather will remain fine. Deviations are unquestionably warnings of change: look out! On passage you can easily sail out of a high or low and then of course the atmospheric pressure on board changes, but without a change in the weather. Superimposed on the normal atmospheric pressure wave of an undisturbed day in the tropics or subtropics there is, however, a tendency for which the atmosphere is not responsible.

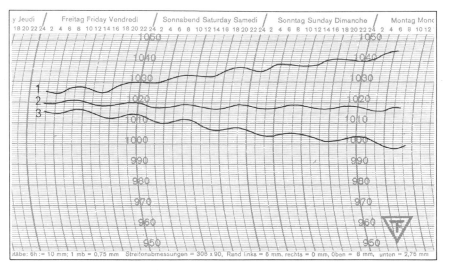

The daily pattern of atmospheric pressure

1. This is the curve recorded on a yacht that sailed into a high, without any change in the weather.

2. Here the rise and fall of the atmospheric 'tide' is shown. The tidal range is ±1.5 mb. The fine weather continues unchanged.

3. And here is the curve recorded by a yacht that sailed out of a high. Although the pressure has dropped considerably the weather remains stable, the daily cycle continuing undisturbed.

This cirrus merely simulates the arrival of a front. In the Med it usually derives from high cumulus. However if the cirrus thickens after noon, caution is necessary and the development of the weather needs to be watched very carefully.

Fronts in the Mediter-ranean

The front phenomena with their cloud processions, well known in the Atlantic, North Sea and the Baltic, substantially don't exist in the Med. Marked pressure drop ahead of a front is rare. The cloud begins to thicken at the cirrus level to indicate something coming, but just at this point it is possible to go badly wrong in assessing the development of the weather: cirrus in the Med frequently derives from cumulus breaking up. These cloud remains are torn apart by the high altitude wind and last for many hours. The cloud picture generated in this way merely looks deceptively like a warm front arriving.

Cold fronts that cross Spain to penetrate the Med are not easy to recognize; the only sign of their having reached the coast is a sprinkling of cirrus and altocumulus. When the front then moves over the sea again, it becomes active with appalling speed: in a short time powerful cumulus storms develop with thunderstorms embedded in them as well.

● If the barometer falls while layer cloud (stracu and altocumulus) is developing, a bad-weather front is on the way.

● If with that cloud development the atmospheric pressure is not falling, high-pressure influence is about to set in.

Fog and haze

Summer is the season for fog in the Med, but all the same there are only a few really foggy days: statistics show 2 per month. Much more often it will be thick haze. Visibility of around 1 mile or even less persists happily for weeks. The typical situation for this is a marked high which has formed a barrier (inversion layer) above the layer of air next the earth's surface. There is a flat calm on land as well as at sea, and the visibility gets worse every day. If a stable high-pressure formation gets established following a *scirocco*, the moist, hazy air – and with this the poor visibility – is maintained for so long that often a whole holiday is not long enough to get a clear sight of the horizon.

Thunderstorms and precipitation

Particularly in the Med, these two weather phenomena frequently occur together. Typical seasonal variations here derive from the temperature of the sea water. The lowest temperatures of 12° to 15°C are in spring. Then the rapidly increasing solar irradiation produces a distinct phase-shift between the warming-up of the water and that of the land. The sea temperature rises only very slowly, and by autumn when at about 25°C it has reached its maximum the land masses are already well into the cooling-off phase. The explanation of the different warming and cooling rates lies in the enormous heat-storage capacity of the water (as used in the hot water bottle). The season-linked activities of the atmosphere derive from this phase-shift because the sea has its

high summer just when the atmosphere is preparing for winter.

How does this affect the various seasons?

Spring

After the winter has brought a lot of wind to the Med, spring is the time when the weather settles. From as early as March onwards, precipitation becomes an increasingly rare event. However until May there is plenty of wind for exuberant sailing: spring in the Med compares with a moderate summer in the North Sea.

As the water temperature rises the typically stable summer weather pattern – settled warm and dry – for which this region is known quickly establishes itself. Thunderstorms are rare in spring and only occur when there is a breakout of cold polar air with an active cold front extending down to the Med. Along the front, and also in the region of the cold-air inflow behind it, the thunderstorms then form.

Summer

The summertime thunderstorms in the Med are triggered by a pretty unusual process: in *scirocco* weather, the places where you must always reckon with hefty thunderstorms are ones far from the African coast. In other words in the sea area around Sardinia, Corsica, Sicily, Malta and also the Balearics a summertime *scirocco* brings not only wind and rough seas but also thunderstorms with generous precipitation.

On its way across the Med the hot Sahara air picks up more and more

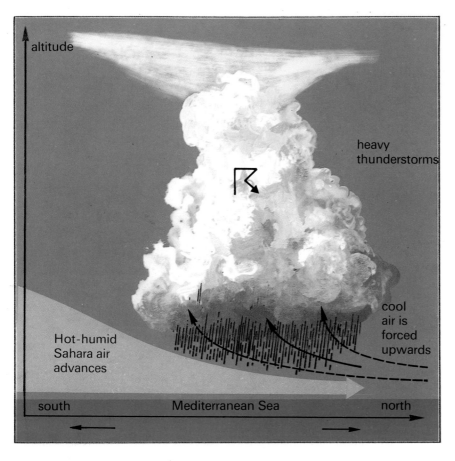

altitude

heavy
thunderstorms

cool
air is
forced
upwards

Hot-humid
Sahara air
advances

south   Mediterranean Sea   north

The Sahara air advancing
towards Italy becomes super-
saturated with moisture and
pushes in underneath the old
Med air. This leads to fierce
thunderstorms with rain
showers.

moisture the farther it advances. In combination with the high temperature of the water this leads to instability of the bottom layer of air, which has become so hot that it shoots upwards at the first opportunity. This produces thunderstorms of a type totally unknown in North Europe. The mass of water falling from the sky is such as to reduce visibility to absolutely zero: it may be a small consolation that this substantially damps-down the seas. Around the Italian coast thunderstorms are mostly *scirocco* linked, if we disregard the evening heat-thunderstorms which in summer can be found everywhere. These are then tied to the vicinity of the warm front, and here the highest level of activity is where this collides with the cold front (occlusion point). Thunderstorms are rarely found in the core-zone of a depression.

The mechanism causing thunderstorms in the northern Adriatic is totally different, and no less interesting, because very suitable for one's own prediction. The Adriatic thunderstorms are coupled to cold-air thrusts across the surrounding mountain ranges and massifs. Cold fronts, even those with little or no effect on the weather in northern or central Europe, turn into the birthplace of really violent tempests if the play of atmospheric forces heaves them across these mountainous barriers. The northern Adriatic, where the water temperature is always high, generates a sort of cloche of warm/hot and always humid air over the whole of the region. If, for example, a cold air mass is shoved across the Alps it won't just plump down again on the other side of the mountain range as one would expect – and as the simple laws of physics imply – but instead will slide over the top of the Adriatic's warm air and so stay at the height to which it was lifted by the obstructing mountains. This is an exceedingly unstable situation and cannot be maintained for long: there

Thunderstorms along cold fronts in the Adriatic

When a cold front crosses the mountain range, at first everything proceeds quite harmlessly. Suddenly, however, the cold air drops right down to the sea and allows the hot, humid sea air to shoot upwards massively resulting in thunderstorms everywhere.

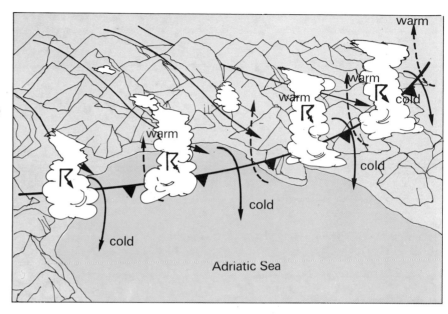

will be an early repositioning of the air masses. Apparently out of nowhere and in what seems a perfectly good high-pressure situation, thunderstorm towers shoot up suddenly and over a large area.

An unpleasant aspect of this type of thunderstorm is that one is surrounded by storms and there is no direction which offers a safe retreat. Often the clouds may form a line, or a horseshoe shape, along the whole inner coast from Grado to Izola; they also like the Gulf of Grado. Thunderstorms are a danger in the Adriatic whenever a cold front passes through, whether it has come over the Alps, the Yugoslav mountains or even those of northern Italy. A useful warning of the early arrival of thunderstorms is the formation of swelling cumulus, particularly if the cloud starts towering upwards from the altocumulus level.

Another typically thunderstormy situation for the Adriatic is when a

low has formed either in the Gulf of Lions or in that of Genoa and crosses east over Italy. With the warm front it will first get even warmer than before, really muggy, apart from the fact that continuous rain frequently occurs over the whole of northern Italy. The cold air that follows usually does not get rid of the moist and warm air because there is next to no frontal activity. As already described, the cold air simply slides over the warm air underneath and at once you have thundery activity over the whole of the region, triggered by a trifling, barely noticed, cold front.

Autumn

In the open sea in the Med the peak time for thundery activity is undoubtedly autumn, whereas the

inner Adriatic and many coastal regions have thunderstorms most frequently in summer. Two factors produce that autumnal maximum: the water reaches its highest temperatures then, and by this time there are once again well marked fronts that advance down into the Med. Autumn is the season for strong heating from below and already significant cooling from higher level.

Sea conditions

Rough seas are usually caused by front-related strong winds. After they die down swell can last up to 24 hours. The typical weather for unpleasant swell in the western Med is the classic *scirocco* with an African low that extends over the sea and

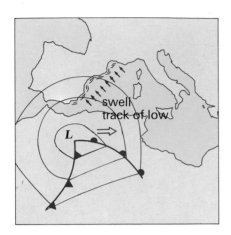

Classic swell-producing situation in the Med.

If with a scirocco the Sahara low moves eastwards, there is a typical swell-producing situation along eastern Spain.

makes its leisurely way eastwards. While this low is moving away it continues to push the seas from the same direction for days on end, so that you get a nasty reinforcement.

The western Med

Along the east coast of Spain down as far as Alicante, northeasterly gales produce the heaviest seas. Southerly gales are dangerous only for a few regions and harbours, because in that direction there is enough protection. Along the southern part of the Spanish coast, it is particularly the east winds that drive a strong swell onto the coast. The hidden cause of this is usually a *scirocco*.

Northwesterly gales have a broad band, probably due to shielding by the coast, without any significant sea. Farther out heavy seas get up quickly. The same applies to the Gulf of Lions where northwesterlies, i.e *mistral*, set up heavy seas beyond where the coast provides a lee. Around Minorca you can reckon with heavy seas and later pronounced swell in strong winds from northwest through north to northeast. Off Corsica, particularly along the west coast south of the island of Sanguinaires, past the Straits of Bonifacio and all along the coast of Sardinia, *mistral* and *mistral*-like conditions generate heavy seas, noticeably heavier than for the wind strength. Seaway conditions when the *libeccio* blows are similarly unfavourable.

Along the French east coast it's the *marin*, a southerly, that brings the heavy seas. Particularly nasty then is the strip of coast from Séte to Aigues-Mortes. In the Gulf of Genoa the *scirocco* is the wind principally

bringing heavy swell to the coast. It often announces its coming by a noticeable rise in the water level. As with a flooding tide, the level quickly rises significantly, then a slowly strengthening swell from the east arrives, and only after that does the wind begin to build up to strong and occasionally even gale force.

The Ionian Sea

It is true to say of the entire Ionian coast that in summer strong winds are pretty rare. However when they do occur, they are associated with very heavy gusts which are long lasting and set up correspondingly heavy seas. In such weather this otherwise peaceful region of the Med is dangerous in the extreme and should as far as possible be avoided. No matter where along the coast you and your yacht are, or even if you are well out on the high seas, they set in with primeval force and in the shortest of time build up mountainous seas. The tendency to gusting is strongest in the evening, and the seaway then the most unpredictable.

The Adriatic

Particularly to the exposed islands off Yugoslavia and the east coast of Italy, the *bora* brings nasty sea waves and swell. The harbours and anchorages on the eastern side of islands and bays are often totally unprotected against the seaway this generates. Anyone lying in one of these harbours in a hefty *bora* is helplessly

Mediterranean Radio Weather Services in English

Country/station	Frequency kHz	Times GMT *Indicates 1 hr. early when daylight saving time in force	Forecast area
Gibraltar			
BFBS	Ch. 1 (93.5, 97.8 Mhz)	0745, 0845, 1306, 1803 Sat: 0745, 0845, 1306 Sun: 0910 *	Radius of 50 miles
ZDK	2598, 2792, Ch. 01–04, 23–25, 27, 28, 86, 87	0000, 0600, 1200, 1800	
France			
Monaco	4363.6	0803, 1303, 1715	Western Med. Northern half (See map. p. 155)
	8728.2	0715, 1715	
	Ch. 23	0730–2400	Western Med.
Italy (See map, p. 156)			
Cagliara (Sardinia)	1722, Ch. 25	0135, 0735, 1135, 1935	Central & South Tyrrenian, Sea of Sardinia & Channel of Sardinia
Porto Torres	1806, Ch. 26	0150, 0750, 1350, 1950	Sea of Corsica, of Sardinia & Central Tyrrenian
Genova	2642, Ch. 25–27	0135, 0735, 1335, 1935	N. Tyrrenian, Ligurian Sea & Sea of Corsica
Livorno	2591, Ch. 26	0135, 0735, 1335, 1935	N. & Central Tyrrenian & Ligurian Sea
Civitavecchia	1888, Ch. 27	0135, 0735, 1335, 1935	N., Central & S. Tyrrenian
Napoli	2635, Ch. 25 & 27	0135, 0735, 1335, 1935	Central & S. Tyrrenian
Messina	2789, Ch. 25	0135, 0735, 1335, 1935	N. & S. Ionian & S. Tyrrenian
Palermo	1705, Ch. 27	0135, 0735, 1335, 1935	Sicily Channel & S. Tyrrenian
Augusta	2628, Ch. 26	0150, 0750, 1350, 1950	Sicily Channel & S. Ionian
Crotone	2663, Ch. 25	0150, 0750, 1350, 1950	N. & S. Ionian
Bari	2579, Ch. 26–27	0135, 0735, 1335, 1935	S. Adriatic & N. Ionian
S. Benedetto Del Tronto	1855	0150, 0750, 1350, 1950	N. & Central Adriatic
Trieste	2624, Ch. 25	0135, 0735, 1335, 1935	N. & Central Adriatic
Yugolsavia			
Rijeka	2771, Ch. 24	0535, 1435, 1935	Adriatic & Strait of Otranto
Split	2685, Ch. 28	0545, 1245, 1945	Adriatic & Strait of Otranto
Dubrovnik	2615, Ch. 04, 25	0625, 1320, 2120	Adriatic & Strait of Otranto
Malta	2625, Ch. 4	0603, 1003, 1603, 2103	Radius of 50 miles
Greece **Helas**			
(stations – see almanac)	Ch. 23–28	on request	Eastern Med.
Kerkyra	2830	0140, 0540, 0940, 1740, 2140	Map opp. Areas B–1
Iraklion (Crete)	2799	0703, 0903, 1533, 2133	Mapp. opp. Areas C, D, I, J & 1–17
Rodos	2624	0703, 0903, 1533, 2133	Map opp. Areas I–M & 1–17
Athenai	2590 8759.2	0703, 0903, 1503, 2103	Map opp. Areas C, D, I, J & 1–17
Hellenic Radio	729, 927, 1008, 1044, 1404, 1485, 1494, 1512	0430, 1330	Med. All areas
Khios	1820	0703, 0903, 1533, 2133	Map opp. Areas I, J & 1–17
Limnos	2730	0703, 0903, 1533, 2133	Map opp. Areas 1–11
Turkey	Ch. 67	0900, 1200, 1500, 1800*	Turkish Coastal waters
Syria			
Lattaquie	2100	0900, 1700	Syrian coastal waters

caught in a mousetrap: the swell often causes heavy damage. Sailing in time and riding out the gale at sea are then not only less stressful for the nerves but also suit the boat better, provided it is seaworthy.

The *scirocco*, which in the Adriatic blows roughly parallel with the coast, in the northern part generates heavy seas everywhere along it. It can frequently be observed that a *scirocco* announces itself by significant swell rolling in from the east before the wind begins to blow from the southeast. In the Po Delta you get the so-called *furiani*: line-squalls from the southeast which come as a complete surprise and set up rough seas.

The Aegean

Strong winds from the north can occur at any time in the year, and have to be allowed for since they intrude into passage planning power-

fully and relentlessly. Only a few hours of blow from the north suffice to set up short, steep and rugged seas between the islands, which can become dangerous. In such weather do avoid passages between islands, especially those between large islands. On the leeward side of these passages you will encounter the most vicious of down-gusts. In such northerlies, stay well away from the islands – the farther away you are, the steadier will be wind and sea.

In the south, around Kythera, it's the winds from the west that build up rugged seas. Even in summer the sea here can be so heavy that you can't enter any of the harbours.

The North African coast

Along the Algerian and Tunisian coasts, west to northwest winds bring uncomfortable seas similar to those along Sardinia. On top of that, the

wind along the African coast is pretty gusty particularly in summer, making for nasty seas. *Mistral* spells with the winds/gales from the NNW often announce themselves by way of the well-known anticipatory swell.

Around Tripoli, throughout the summer half-year you have to reckon with occasional gusty spells which rapidly raise steep seas.

Shipping bulletins for the Med

Although the Med has a multitude of stations regularly sending out weather reports, many skippers still feel badly looked after, particularly newcomers to the region. The reasons for this contradiction are twofold. First, the language barrier, a major obstacle that cannot be overlooked: too many different languages are spoken. The hope of hearing a report that is first transmitted in the local language being regularly repeated in the universal language, English, is unfortunately realized all too infrequently. A second deficiency concerns the forecast areas of the local radio stations, which mostly don't extend beyond their own environs. So you can't really plan a passage using a single weather bulletin. The alternative is to take down a shipping bulletin that, say, covers all the sea areas of the western Med. Unfortunately with these generalised forecasts for vast areas the skipper loses the especially important detailed information and the local weather peculiarities. How can this problem be tackled?

The one and only solution to this dilemma for the foreseeable future is weather fax. Independent of all languages and limitations of area, one gets on board in an understandable form all that's necessary. I don't think there is a lot of point in listing all the frequencies, transmission times and stations around the Med that send out weather reports because particularly in this field a lot is currently changing. Annual listings in *Reed's Mediterranean Almanac* are useful, as are those in the *Macmillan & Silk Cut Almanac*.

The weather map on the right and that at the bottom of page 154 show forecast areas used by the Hamburg German language broadcasts for the Mediterranean.

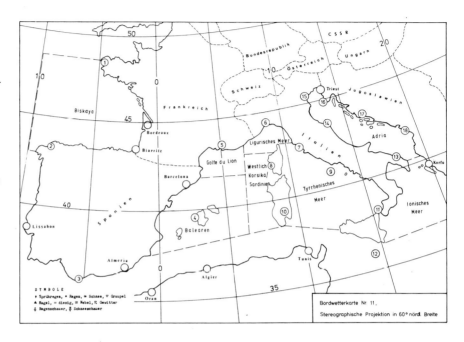

Areas covered by Greek forecasts (in English)

Coastal waters

1	Saronicos	10	Samos Sea
2	S Evvocios	11	Thrakiko
3	Thermaicos	12	Kos-Rodos Sea
4	Korinthiacos	13	W Karpathio
5	Patraicos	14	E Karpathio
6	NW Aegean	15	E Kretan
7	NE Aegean	16	W Kretan
8	SW Aegean	17	Kithira Sea
9	SE Aegean		

Sea areas
A North Adriatic
B South Adriatic
C North Ionian Sea
D South Ionian Sea
E Boot
F Melita
G Gabes
H Sidra

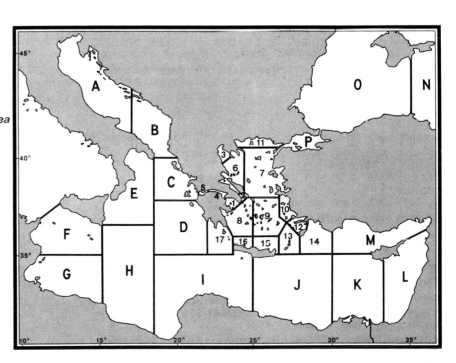

155

Wind strengths in various languages

Wind strength Beaufort scale	Danish	Norwegian	Swedish	English
0	stille	stille	stiltje	calm
1	flov brise	flau vind	nästan stiltje	light air
2	let brise	svak vind	lätt bris	light breeze
3	jävn brise	lett bris	god bris	gentle breeze
4	frisk brise	laber bris	frisk bris	moderate breeze
5	kuling	frisk bris	styv bris	fresh breeze
6	stiv kuling	liten kuling	hård bris	strong breeze
7	hard kuling	stiv kuling	styv kultje	moderate gale
8	stormende kuling	sterk kuling	hård kultje	fresh gale
9	storm	liten storm	halv storm	strong gale
10	svär storm	full storm	storm	whole gale
11	orkanagtig storm	sterk storm	svår storm	storm
12	orkan	orkan	orkan	hurricane

Areas covered by French forecasts (in French/English)

513 = Nord Baléares	**531 = Gênes**
521 = Lion	**532 = Ouest Corse**
522 = Provence	**533 = Est Corse**
523 = Ouest Sardaigne	

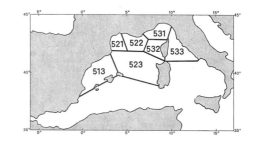

Wind strength Beaufort scale	Dutch	French	Spanish	Italian
0	stilte	calme	calma	calma
1	flauw én stil	très légère brise	ventolina	bavi di vento
2	flauwe koelte	légère brise	brisa débil, flojito	brezza leggera
3	lichte koelte	petite brise	brisa débil, flojo	brezza fesa
4	matige koelte	jolie brise	bonancible, brisa moderate	vento moderato
5	frisse bries	bonne brise	brisa fresca	vento feso
6	stijve bries	vent frais	brisa fuerte, fresco	vento fresco
7	harde wind	grand frais	viento fuerte, frescachón	vento forte
8	stormachtig	coup de vent	viento duro, viento atemporalado	burrasca
9	storm	fort coup de vent	viento muy duro, temporal	burrasca forte
10	zware storm	tempête	temporal fuerte	tempesta
11	zeer zware storm	violente tempête	temporal huracando	tempesta violenta
12	orkaan	ouragan	huracán	uragano

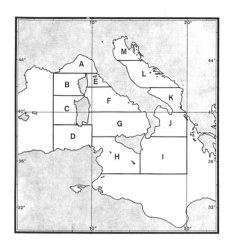

Areas covered by Italian fore-casts (in English)

A   Mar Ligure
B   Mar di Corsica
C   Mar di Sardegna
D   Canale di Sardegna
E   Tirreno settentrionale
F   Tirreno centrale
G   Tirreno meridionale
H   Canale di Sicilia
I   Ionio meridionale
J   Ionio settentrioinale
K   Adriatico meridionale
L   Adriatico centrale
M   Adriatico settentrionale

Mediterranian Radio Weather Services				
Country/station	Language	Frequency kHz	Times GMT *indicates 1 hr early when daylight saving time in force	Forecast area
Spain				
Cabo de la Nao	Spanish	1690	1103, 1733	Western Med.
St. Lys Radio	Spanish	4328, 6421.5	0750, 1600	Western Med.
France				
Marseille	French	1906, Ch. 24, 26, 28	0103, 0705, 1220, 1615 on request	French coast & Corsica
Fos	French	Ch. 28	0633, 1133	French coast & Corsica
France-Inter	French	164	0655, 2005*	All French areas
Ajaccio	French	Ch. 24	0733, 1233*	French coast & Corsica
Italy				
Radiotelevisione Italiana-Radiodue	Italian	846, 936, 1035, 1116, 1118, 1314, 1431, 1449	0600, 1445, 2145* Sun: 0600, 1545, 2145*	All Italian areas
Tunis	French	1820, 2670, 2182	0805, 1305, 1705	Tunisia, N. & E. coastal
Algeria	French	890, 11715, 1304	1300, 2000	Western Med.

Index

Useful telephone nos.

Marinecall

Provides latest weather forecasts for
each area as supplied by the Met.
Office. Dial 0898 500 followed by the
desired area code. This is a 24 hr.
Service.

Area	Code
1	451
2	452
3	453
4	454
5	455
6	456
7	457
8	458
9	459
10	460
11	461
12	462
13	463
14	464
15	465

Forecasts for local weather from the following – ask for 'Forecast Office'

N.E. England 091 232 6453
N.W. England 061 477 1060
E. England 0603 66 0779
S.E. England 071 836 4311
S. England 0703 22 8844
S.W. England 0752 40 2534
W. England 0272 27 9298
N. Ireland 084 94 22339
W. & S.E. Scotland 041 248 3451

France
Boulogne (21) 33.82.55
Deauville (31) 88.84.22
Dinard (99) 46.18.77
Brest (98) 84.82.83
Marseille (91) 91.46.51
St. Tropez (94) 97.23.57
Nice (93) 83.17.24